Setting Up and Facilitating Student-Centered Classrooms

Sandra J. Phifer

A Scarecrow Education Book
The Scarecrow Press, Inc.
Lanham, Maryland, and London
2002

A SCARECROW EDUCATION BOOK

Published in the United States of America
by Scarecrow Press, Inc.
A Member of the Rowman & Littlefield Publishing Group
4720 Boston Way, Lanham, Maryland 20706
www.scarecroweducation.com

4 Pleydell Gardens, Folkestone
Kent CT 20 2DN, England

British Library Cataloging in Publication Information Available

Library of Congress Cataloging-in-Publication Data

Phifer, Sandra J.
  Setting up and facilitating student-centered classrooms / Sandra J. Phifer.
    p. cm.
  Includes bibliographical references (p.).
  ISBN 0-8108-4192-4 (pbk. : alk. paper)
  1. Classroom management. 2. Teaching. 3. Learning. I. Title.
LB3013.P46 2002
371.102'4—dc21

2001049210

Contents

Preface

I was blessed to have parents who raised their children using methods to develop individual strengths and encourage responsibility and independence without the fear of punishment. I was not one of those children who "always wanted to be a teacher," although reading, doing puzzles, and learning new things were some favorite activities.

My interest in facilitating the learning of young children really blossomed when I had a daughter. Then, I was fortunate to be able to work cooperatively with innovative and creative principals and teachers. Professors at the University of Nebraska prompted further investigation into how humans learn during my doctoral studies. All the children and parents in my teaching experiences in Nebraska and Virginia offered great learning opportunities to determine how to best facilitate learning for students of varied populations and learning strengths and differences. I have spent the last six years at Fort Hays State University working with students in a field-based teacher preparation program, and am currently at Metro State College of Denver teacher preparation program.

I want to thank my family, teachers, coworkers, and students who have helped me be a lifelong learner. Thanks to those who provided encouragement and ideas for writing this book and to those who contributed samples of their work: Bryce Woodall (graphics), Tamara Padfield (song), and T. J. Trout (peer assessment forms).

I want to encourage all educators to work and collaborate with other educators at all levels of experience and interests. Teachers are very generous and will share ideas, experiences, and ideas to promote learning. I know some people tell teaches to "steal" from other teachers; I encourage you to "borrow and share" ideas. Let teachers know when you think they have good ideas and methods; this is a compliment, and teachers need positive affirmations that they are competent professionals who are appreciated.

Introduction

Congratulations! If you are reading this book, you are probably embarking upon one of the most challenging and satisfying of all careers—that of a teacher. Teaching has always been an influential position, and continues to become even more consequential in our changing society. Teachers affect the lives of countless young people and are frequently the primary source of stability and positive encouragement to foster development of each and every student.

You undoubtedly like and respect all young people and believe that every child can be a successful learner and decision-maker. You want to establish a classroom that will cultivate development of life skills in every one of these students. It is hoped you have been able to observe and work with other teachers who share your beliefs and desire to achieve a learning environment where students are actively and eagerly engaged in learning. You know that you have a gigantic job ahead to plan and organize to effectively facilitate the learning environment to reach the goals of all students. This book is meant to provide a guide in your momentous quest. You are invited to personally contact me with further questions, suggestions, or to brainstorm specific problems you encounter. I can be reached at phifers@mscd.edu or pinephifer@quest.net.

1

Teacher Beliefs, Expectations, and Learning Goals

A smooth sea never made a skilled mariner.
English proverb

Teaching is an honored profession that has great influence on the future of our country. It is expected that approximately two-thirds of America's teaching staff will be replaced. Most would agree that the teacher has the greatest influence on student attitude and student achievement than any other factor in school. What an opportunity to re-create America's schools and the teaching profession!

Effective schools of the future will focus on creating places that engage students and inviting students to be involved in meaningful learning activities. These activities must challenge students to use complex thinking and problem solving connected to relevant, reality-based life experiences.

This book is directed toward practicing teachers or those who are preparing to be future teachers who realize that teaching extends beyond presenting knowledge to students and "telling students how they should act." The teachers believe that students must be active participants in the teaching-learning processes and that students construct knowledge based on their own perceptions of the events.

- All students in the classroom have the ability to learn; however, all students will not learn in the same way or at the time.

- Students will not have all the same background experiences; consequently, students may require more or fewer readiness experiences.

- Developmental levels of students will influence perceptions and interpretations of personal learning experiences.

- Learning occurs in a social environment; the school and classrooms and the home cultural environments all influence student learning.

- Learners are whole people; cognitive learning cannot be separated from social and emotional components of the person.

LEARNING GOALS FOR STUDENTS

Learning goals for students focus on gaining the knowledge, skills, and strategies to be successful learners and citizens today and in the future. These goals might be stated in any of the following statements.

- Chinese proverb: Give a fish, live for a day; teach to fish, live for life.

- Facilitate independence, and the ability to think and care for self.

- Become an effective problem-solver of learning and social problems.

- Know how to be a continuous learner; how to access and evaluate new information.

- Attain personal awareness of own skills and learning strengths and needs.

- Learn basic skills of reading, writing, speaking, listening, math concepts.

- Skills and attitudes to be successful citizens of U.S. include self-responsibility and social interaction skills.

TEACHER EXPECTATIONS OF STUDENTS

Teachers need to share their expectations with students. These expectations should form the foundation for determining the structure of the environment and learning program. There must be daily consistency to achieve goals.

- Students must believe they are worthy and can learn.

- Students will be actively involved in own learning; asking questions, seeking answers.

- Students will put forth effort to learn for own benefit. Learning cannot be done for someone else.

- Students will respect self, other students, and adults.

- Students are empowered to make personal choices; they will not be "bossed" by others.

- Students will accept responsibility for all their behaviors (implies being truthful).

- Students will be responsible for own belongings and treat others' belongings with respect.

- Students and teachers will make mistakes; mistakes are part of the learning process.

2

Student Characteristics Influence Learning

Who you are speaks so loudly I can't hear what you are saying.
Ralph Waldo Emerson

Learning results from the interaction of biological qualities and life experiences of each student. The amount and quality of life personal experiences affect how new experiences will be perceived and interpreted. The social experiences of each student will affect all cognitive interpretations. Children's social environments usually expand as children age; therefore, the interpretations of these experiences will have some basic characteristics usually common within particular age groups. The characteristics that will most affect the teaching and learning needs within these age groups are noted below.

EARLY CHILDHOOD STUDENT CHARACTERISTICS

- Child is active explorer, discover; "why" and "how come" questions drive actions toward discovery.

- Play is the preferred method of learning.

- Pretend and make-believe are just as viable as reality; if the child can "see," it's real.

- Repetition, with variations, is desired; children may want to read same book, play same game over and over.

- Language development is key to cognition; language is learned readily in early years through life exposures.

- Rote learning comes easily, but doesn't mean the underlying concepts are understood (for example, can count and say alphabet but doesn't understand "numberness of concept of amount" or sounds and uses of letters of the alphabet).

- Interpretations of experiences are quite literal and from each individual's perceptions and view (listen to words the child says to get insight into child's interpretation of words or experience).

- Muscles still developing; gross motor movements are more developed than smaller muscles in extremities; children are still learning to put actions together fluidly (step-hop for skip). Girls tend to be more advanced in motor development and coordination during early years.

- Children need active movement frequently (do not need to be still be listen and think). Movement increases the heart rate and blood circulation to all parts of the body, including the brain.

- Young children have more brain activity and more synaptic connections; these are refined and pruned with experience. Attention spans are short; hands-on activities will hold attention longer than auditory or visual only.

- Social skills of sharing and turn-taking are difficult due to egocentricism; these skills need to be modeled, practiced, and encouraged.

- Young children tend to believe that parents and teachers "know" everything. They haven't always understood that everyone makes mistakes, and that differences of opinion are common.

MIDDLE CHILDHOOD (8–12)

- World is expanding; friends are becoming increasing more important.
  - Girls tend to want a "best friend" (may change on frequent basis) or small group of friends.
  - Boys tend to have larger groups of friends, often activity or sports oriented.
  - Interest in other gender evident at end of this age span.
- Girls may be more physically mature than boys; increasing numbers of girls experience first menarche during this age span.
- Thinking ability is more logical, but continues to need "hands-on" experiences to really understand and make sense of concept.
- Children can use multiple attributes to classify and sort concepts (color, size, shape, use, etc.).
- Most can understand and follow rules of games and activities.
- Some children are developing the ability to think in abstract (particularly in areas/topics have had many experiences).

ADOLESCENCE (13–18)

- Puberty (and time of onset) is greatest factor in social-emotional development of individuals. Children who experience puberty much earlier or later than peers may have social and emotional repercussions.

- Students are establishing independence and identity as an individual; this is often accompanied by behaviors that appear to look rebellious (think of them as two-year-olds with greater latitudes).

- Adolescents tend to believe that "everyone" is looking at and talking about them.

- Friends provide feedback and focus for standards of what they should say and how to act in social world.

- Increasing number of pupils are gaining ability to think in abstract; however, the majority are still concrete thinkers.

INTELLECTUAL AND COGNITIVE LEARNING DIFFERENCES

Students have a wide variance in learning experiences, preferences, and abilities; every child has his/her own unique brain activity. The brain is still quite flexible; varied experiences will promote connections between parts of the brain as well as "pruning" and organizing synapsis for more efficient processing.

ENVIRONMENTAL FACTORS

Dunn and Dunn identified a number of environmental, emotional, sociological, and physical factors that may affect the comfort level of the learner. These include lighting, time of day one operates most effectively, learning "places," groupings, and room arrangement.

- Teachers can plan the environment and learning to meet individual needs of students through various methods.

  - Arrange physical environment to provide places, for students to work individually, in small groups, with or without direct supervision, quiet places and places for discussions, places with minimal distractions, and more informal, lounging places.

— Learning objectives should be clear, but offer choices at varying levels of competency.

— Choices of learning activities for objectives should include multiple methods to learn and how learning is demonstrated (assessment).

— Include individual, pair, and small group/team self-checks and assessments.

— Provide opportunities for team and small group work and seminars.

PERCEPTUAL MODES

Perceptual modes refers to the senses that attend and "take in" information from the environment. The goal would be to provide learning /information for multiple senses to focus.

- Auditory

  — Learns best through verbal communications.

  — Problem solves by talking through problem and solutions (aloud or by subvocalizing).

  — Uses auditory decoding strategies; uses phonetic approach to spell.

- Visual

  — Learns best by seeing and demonstrations.

  — Makes notes and lists, pictures.

  — Visualizes, good imagery; reads and spells by word configurations.

- Kinesthetic

  — Learns best by direct involvement, by doing.

  — Often an impulsive problem-solver; wants to actively try out solutions.

  — May be poor speller and indifferent reader (unless actions involved).

DIFFERENCES IN VIEW OF INTELLIGENCE

The traditional view of intelligence focused on students who scored high on "intelligence tests" and in assigned schoolwork. Both methods favored students who had good vocabulary and language skills and logical mathematical problem-solving abilities. Other students may have been viewed by teachers and parents as being more capable than their learning work/products reflected. Alternative views of intelligence propose that intelligence extends beyond the abilities of language and logical thinking. If intelligence is viewed as the capacity or ability to think, reason, acquire, and apply knowledge, then it seems logical that an individual's brain would not have identical "pathways" established to facilitate problems in identical ways.

ROBERT STERNBERG'S TRIARCHY MODEL OF INTELLIGENCE

Sternberg views intelligence as a set of abilities required for the individual to achieve success in meeting expectations of the individual and others. It is important that each individual recognize and use individual strengths to make adjustments and adaptations to self or the environment to achieve success.

- *Analytical ability* includes the ability to analyze, compare and contrast, and evaluate problems. This ability best corresponds to intelligence as the student who scores high on intelligence tests and other conventional types of classroom tests and assignments.

- *Creative ability* is the ability to create, invent, and discover ideas that are novel and valuable; it is both an ability and an attitude. Young children more frequently display creative ideas and abilities; society often forces conformity, thereby suppressing creative thinking.

- *Practical ability is* when one applies or uses what has been learned. It includes the ability to learn by one's mistakes. The individual must be able to identify personal strengths and have the motivation and other personal attributes to tackle and successfully meet the problems of life.

- Sternberg emphasizes the importance of teaching and assessing triarchically (TIA). TIA stresses the importance of diversity and uniqueness of learners.

  — Use materials in teaching-learning that will capitalize on all abilities and promote the development of all three abilities.

  — Help students become aware of their strengths and how to use their strengths to compensate for weaker thinking and skill areas.

  — Enhance student motivation for learning by allowing students to demonstrate their individuality and knowledge.

For additional information and methods for TIA, see Sternberg, R. J. & E. Grigorenko (2000), *Teaching for Successful Intelligence to Increase Student Learning and Achievement*, Andover, MA: SkyLight Training and Publishing, Inc.

HOWARD GARDNER'S MODEL OF MULTIPLE INTELLIGENCES

Gardner expanded the concept of intelligence to include abilities that are valued within a culture. Gardner believes intelligence can be exhibited in multiple ways and that these abilities or intelligences can be developed. Gardner believes that we all possess all intelligences, but usually one or two are more highly developed in individuals that others. Eight intelligences (more are possible) have been identified and developed in Gardner's Multiple Intelligence interpretation.

1. *Verbal-Linguistic Intelligence:* ability to use words and language for various purposes. Individuals with high verbal-linguistic intelligence learn best by speaking, listening, reading, or writing.

2. *Logical-Mathematical Intelligence:* ability to find patterns, sequence, see relationships and cause-effect.

3. *Spatial Intelligence:* capacity for perceiving, creating, and re-creating pictures and images and have keen sense of location and direction.

4. *Musical Intelligence:* ability to respond to or produce melody and rhythm of music and everyday sounds.

5. *Bodily-Kinesthetic Intelligence:* abilities related to awareness and manipulation of own body.

6. *Interpersonal Intelligence:* abilities related to social competence and interactions with others; includes being able to gauge, empathize, and react to others in positive methods.

7. *Intrapersonal Intelligence:* abilities to access own inner feelings, needs, goals.

8. *Naturalistic Intelligence:* abilities to respond to patterns and features of the natural environment; tends to have deep understanding and appreciation for environment, natural objects, and living things.

Gardner's model has many implications and applications to educational programs. Teachers can provide teaching-learning activities and assessments to utilize and develop all the intelligences. Multiple resources provide specific methods and activities to utilize multiple intelligence in planning learning activities and assessments.

• To help all students learn successfully, teachers can incorporate multiple intelligences in planning lessons by using numerous methods or giving choices in the materials of presentation, practice, or assessment activities.

— oral and written language, include literature, life stories, and examples;

— visuals aids and organizers;

— environmental or language musical lyrics or rhythms;

— body movements or kinesthetic tactile activities;

— logical categorizing, patterning, critical thinking;

— natural living environment;

— students' personal feelings, memories, interests;

— work with partner, cooperative learning, group discussions.

RESOURCES

Campbell, L., B. Campbell, and D. Dickinson. *Teaching and Learning through Multiple Intelligences.* Needham Heights, MA: 1999.

Gardner, H. *Multiple Intelligence: The Theory in Practice.* New York: Basic Books, 1993.

Kagan, S., and M. Kagan. *Multiple Intelligences: The Complete MI Book.* San Clemente, CA: Kagan Cooperative Learning, 1998.

ENVIRONMENTAL DIFFERENCES

Students are results of their genetic factors and their experiences in life. Therefore, the environment greatly affects what they know, and how they respond to specific instances.

Their language, values, interaction patterns, interests, goals and expectations, and background experiences (including educational) are all related to environmental factors.

SOCIAL-ECONOMIC STATUS

Because social-economic status affects almost all of the noted "difference factors," social-economic status has the greatest effect on educational goals and success, and is the variable most used to compare educational outcomes. Be aware that social-economic status extends beyond the amount of income; equally important are educational status, and personal factors that influence where the family lives, types of life experiences and interactions, and the opportunities for gainful employment.

Specific factors that have educational implications are:

- Health factors (diet, exposure of medical assistance, environmental exposure to toxins, etc.).

- Language interaction patterns of the home environment (vocabulary, dialect, rhythm of language, directives and put-downs versus positive explanations).

- Parental encouragement to explore, question, and problem solve.

- Values in life (what is important, goals to work toward).

- Modeling and encouragement of adults in home.

- Exposure to life experiences in expanding social world with explanations and encouragement to question and understand "the why's" of their world.

Teachers need to be aware of how students' experiences (or lack of) will influence learning, motivation, and behaviors. Teachers should not confuse the lack of prior knowledge or experiences with ability to learn; teachers may need to be prepared to provided background experiences to permit students to be successful in their learning. Educators should work to form community-home-school connections with these families.

INCLUSION OF EXCEPTIONAL STUDENTS IN CLASSROOM

The student-centered classroom is structured around the concept that all students can and will learn. It is assumed that diversity exists in students' background knowledge and individual learning strengths and needs, including those identified as exceptional students. The student-centered classroom is frequently the optimum learning situation for most of these students. Exceptional students are viewed as students who learn differently from others, not as students who have weaknesses or disabilities and can't learn.

- Choices are offered for varying learning needs and levels.

- Students learn from one another in heterogeneous, student-centered classrooms.

- Special students and regular students grow in social acceptance of differences.

- Special students usually make significant gains in cognitive learning.

- Classroom teachers and special education personnel work together as a team to teach all students in the classroom.

3

Getting Yourself Ready for Success

Know thyself, for once we know ourselves, we may learn
how to care for ourselves, but otherwise we never shall.
Socrates

LOOK IN THE MIRROR

Everything about the teacher is observed by students all day long; the teacher is automatically placed in the role of model. It is hoped this role is a positive example of how a professional person should look and sound. Teachers' confidence level can be enhanced when they are perceived as "looking and acting" like a professional person.

- Determine what lines and colors look best on you.

  — Consult an expert (not clerk selling clothes).

  — Drape material of varying colors and hues around shoulders; see which enhance color or drain from your skin tones.

  — Stand in front of mirror and try on different styles of clothing.

  — Determine which lines and styles makes you feel and look best.

- Look professional; don't compete with adolescent fads.

  — Make certain you are covered in areas that may make you or students uncomfortable if exposed. Remember that you will be sitting, standing, bending down, etc. Check all positions.

  — Clothing should fit and have room to move comfortably.

  — Teachers spend much of the day on their feet. Make certain shoes are comfortable and neat.

— Select a basic color to start your clothing wardrobe (including shoes).

— Add pieces in your "best" colors that go next to your face (shirts, ties, scarves, etc.).

— Jackets emphasize the professional look.

— Pockets are very handy!

— Don't be afraid to accessorize; jewelry, scarves, ties add color and interest. Accessories should always be comfortable and shouldn't be "getting in the way."

— You might want to keep smock or cover-up available for "messy" activities.

— Keep clothing clean and pressed.

• Personal hygiene is important.

— Find a hairstyle that's easy to keep clean and neat.

— Smells are important. Remember that odors cling to clothing and hair.

— Keep colognes and perfumes subtle.

— Don't forget to check your breath! You might want to keep breath enhancers and bottled water handy.

CHECK COMMUNICATION

• Listen to yourself. Make audio of yourself speaking—perhaps leading a lesson.

— Are you speaking too fast? Too slow?

— Do you use run-on sentences?

— Do you use numerous "ers, ahs," etc.?

— Does your enunciation support and enhance your verbal message?

— Do you pause after important concepts and after asking questions?

— Do you allow others to speak without interrupting?

— Check grammar and word pronunciation.

• Watch yourself teaching a lesson.

— Do your eyes and mouth both smile?

— Check your nonverbal facial expressions. Does your face correspond to the verbal messages?

— Do you have any nervous movements that detract from your message?

— If you have problems with your hands, find a place to keep them quiet (clasp together, put in pocket).

— Check your listening postures. Does it appear that you are really interested in what others are saying?

— Do you look natural and relaxed?

GET ORGANIZED

Organizing your personal and professional time and materials will assist your efforts to reduce stress and promote effectiveness. A significant role of the teacher in the student-centered learning environment involves planning and organizing activities and materials so students can be successful independent learners.

CREATE A SCHEDULE FOR YOURSELF

• Extend time frames beyond hours of actual classes. Look at your entire day.

• Put in all activities and responsibilities that you know in advance or that occur on a regular cycle.

• Remember to allow time for your own and family time requirements. You need to stay healthy, so exercise, relaxing, meals, and sleep are important.

• A teacher usually has requirements beyond actual classroom and teaching needs (meetings, committees, professional organizations, and extracurricular activities).

• You will need blocks of time for planning and record keeping. Some schools provide time during the week, but you may need to find additional time. Try to schedule these activities when you work most efficiently. (Sunday at 10 P.M. is not recommended!)

ORGANIZE YOUR MATERIALS AT HOME AND SCHOOL

- Have designated spaces for your things—clothes, keys, bills, etc.—and then remember to put them there! Don't waste time searching for things.

- Help organize and schedule responsibilities for family and students. Your responsibility is to help young people become independent individuals. They can't meet these goals if someone does everything for them.

- Use a designated, labeled place for learning materials that students will be using on a consistent basis.

- Store materials not currently needed in container with labels that can easily be read and retrieved. Dividers and labels reduce time searching and retrieving.

- Find a way to reduce and coordinate all paper teaching materials (ideas, lesson plans, etc.) so you can quickly find and use. You might consider scanning into computer storage system.

- Teachers have to keep lots of records. It is hoped most of these are already on a computer or can be converted to the computer. Check this out.

4

Planning the Learning Environment

Life is a succession of lessons which must
be lived to be understood.
Helen Keller

THE PHYSICAL ENVIRONMENT

The physical environment or teaching-learning "space" is usually determined before a teacher is hired. Although there are variances on what is provided, most classrooms usually have some common attributes: walls are usually painted and are seldom constructed of sound-absorbing material but usually have some bulletin boards and some type of writing board; flooring will most likely be tile or industrial carpet or a combination of the two; lighting is most likely from fluorescent ceiling lights, though many rooms may also have natural lighting from windows. There will probably also be some type of shelving or storage. Electrical outlets are another important entity that will affect room arrangement and usage.

How does one take the givens and create an effective learning environment? Considerations during the planning process include:

- The physical environment structure (noted above); can any be altered?

- Checking with administrative policy and head custodian on regulations regarding safety requirements and possible additions or alterations you may desire; for example, additional electrical outlets may be requisitioned.

- Will you be the only or primary teacher in this space?

- What type of activities do you plan to incorporate? Will you need space for large group, small group, and individual activities?

- Are storage places for teaching-learning supplies near the place where the activity will occur and will readily be accessible to students?

- What type of storage is available for teacher supplies and materials that are not used on a daily basis and for materials that will be used consistently?

- What type of furniture is available (desks/tables, etc.)? Are there possibilities to trade or change any of the furniture? Let other teachers know what you have and would like to trade.

ARRANGING THE ROOM FOR EFFECTIVE TEACHING-LEARNING ACTIVITIES

- Entrance and exit pathways from room should be clear and unobstructed.

- If students will be wearing or bringing personal items (coats, bookbags, etc.), a place near the door will facilitate drop-off and pick-up.

- Teacher desk or personal workspace should be in out-of-way back or side area as this space will not be utilized during teaching-learning times.

- If water is available in room, place work center/activities that will need water in this area.

- Position low storage holders (can also divide work areas) by activity center where materials will be used. Provide labels (words and/or pictures) so students can locate and return materials.

- Determine area for teacher-led instruction/activities; make certain students will have clear view; that there are facilities for demonstrations, writing student responses, and electrical outlets.

WALLS AND BULLETIN BOARDS

- Consider adding materials on walls, dividers, etc., that will help absorb sounds.

- Develop a theme to tie teaching-learning activities to room atmosphere and group cohesion. The physical environment provides clues to excite students about upcoming learning.

- Prepare wall and bulletin board spaces to facilitate or promote teaching-learning.

- Consider covering bulletin boards with background material that can be left up for all or most of year (like yard goods, felt, burlap, or neutral paper that looks like brown bags).

- Uses for bulletin boards include:

  — Interactive learning activity

  — Ongoing teaching-learning center (calendar, writing center, problem-solving activities)

  — Daily/weekly organizing center

  — Displaying student learning products

  — Resources to promote student learning

- Remember that bulletin boards do not need to be restricted to fit within the borders of the board. Visuals can be added that extend and expand the space.

- Consider adding three-dimensional effects; for example, use actual clothing with some stuffing instead of flat paper cut-outs.

- Remember that all bulletin boards do not need to be totally completed before the students arrive on the first day. Some may have only the background, visuals, and title. Student activities in the first days could focus on materials for the boards (for example, "getting to know us" activities).

- Use ideas that can be changed or altered on a variable schedule so changes do not need to occur at same time.

CREATING AN ATMOSPHERE TO WELCOME STUDENTS

The room can be arranged to facilitate safety and learning, but the physical setting of the environment extends beyond the visual. The environment in student-centered learning must invite the students in and provide the emotional security to expose their thoughts and feelings and take risks to ask questions and provide possible solutions.

- Emotional security involves the interaction of people; in the classroom it starts with the teacher. The teacher can welcome students in a number of ways; consider student characteristics, number of students, and teacher preference in selecting student invitations methods.

  — Call each student at home before the school year begins to introduce yourself and welcome student to the classroom.

  — Send a written welcome (postcards work great) to your students and introduce yourself. A list of required or suggested supplies could also be included.

  — Greet students at door every day. Give verbal or written message to let students know what they are to do next.

SAMPLE OF GET-ACQUAINTED BULLETIN BOARD FOR BEGINNING OF YEAR

Title   Look Who's in Room _____

Graphics   Big googly eyes (could add glasses) looking down from top of bulletin board; looks great if you can extend to eyes beyond the board or make 3D.

Student Individual Sheet Take a picture (or have students use camcorders and do own) of each student.
                          Each student completes the information about self. This could include:

        Name
        Birthday
        Favorites (food, color, school activity, hobbies, or "for fun" activities)
        Four nice things about _____.
        Put heading and leave space at the bottom with lines.

Post sheets and encourage students (and teacher) to write nice things they know or observe about other students. This activity could follow a class meeting/discussion on giving positive messages about a person's character, actions, or abilities.

5

Rules and Procedures

The secret of education lies in respecting the pupil.
Ralph Waldo Emerson

Remember, the goal of a student-centered classroom is for students to be actively involved in activities to promote learning and thinking. Personal independence and learning how to learn are also important goals.

It is the teacher's role to set up the classroom for these goals to be accomplished. Planning begins long before students arrive; during the first days and weeks of the term, the expectations and methods to actualize are shared with students.

SCHEDULES

Some components of schedules are set beyond the classroom (beginning, ending, lunch, other specials). Start with these givens. It is helpful if the schedule can be arranged into larger blocks of times to minimize transitions and allow for flexibility to meet all teaching-learning needs.

- You may need to talk with other teachers to promote the idea of block and cluster scheduling.

  — Focus on how this type of scheduling will maximize student learning and facilitate teacher planning time.

  — High school teachers may have the most difficult time convincing others who have been locked into daily short blocks. Talk to administrators; present plan and rationale (backed by research). Change may need to begin with a pilot group of teachers who desire to integrate or add learning activities that will require longer time periods to accomplish.

- Large blocks provides more opportunity for student input and choices; e.g., where they would prefer breaks, sharing, story, etc.

EXAMPLE OF SCHEDULE

- School Begins
  - Roll; lunch
  - Opening announcements
  - Calendar activities
- Reading-Language Arts Block
  - This would include reading, writing activities
  - Shared reading, mini-lessons, teacher conferences
  - Buddy or group reading or writing shares
  - Skill-building centers or instruction
  - Phases of writing activities from pre-writing through publication
  - Literature or theme extensions
- Lunch Break
- Math and Science Block
- Specials
- Story Time
- Closing Discussion, Dismissal

MIDDLE OR HIGH SCHOOL SCHEDULE CONSIDERATIONS

Traditional Schedules: In educational setting (most middle and secondary settings) where classes rotate teachers every period, students need to know where to go each period and what will happen during each period.

5–10 minutes:	Review activity
10–15 minutes:	Introduction of new concept or objective
20–30 minutes:	Application activities

ALTERNATIVE BLOCK SCHEDULES

Schools are working to change schedules to better meet the needs of students and keep them in school and involved in active, meaningful learning activities. Schools can be creative in designing schedules to best meet their learning goals.

- *Teams:* Teams may be composed of teachers with specialities in different areas who work together with the same group of students.

  — Some schools choose to keep the same group of students for one to three years instead of students and classes by semesters or quarters. Teacher believe it is easier to know students individually and respond to their strengths and needs, and build trusting relationships so social and personal development can be addressed.

- *Home Room:* Students report to same teacher daily for Attendance and Group Building/Problem Solving activities or discussions.

- *Developing Blocks of Time:* There are multiple ways to provide longer blocks of learning times.

  — Blocks are divided so classes meet two or three times per week on alternating schedule.

  — Classes a, b, c, d meet with one group of teachers/classes on Monday and Tuesday, while e, f, g, h meet with another group, then switch for Wednesday and Thursday. Friday could have large blocks for integrations, field experiences, and integration; small group and individual seminars; and special helps and conferences, small group shares, and special club meetings. Focus on keeping students involved and learning on a continuous basis and to keep them interested and motivated to learn.

BELIEFS AND EXPECTATIONS

Teachers have carefully thought through their basic beliefs about students, the goals for learning, and the roles of teacher and students in achieving these goals. Let students know your basic beliefs and goals.

Examples of what might be included:

- Every student is capable of thinking and learning.

- Every student is capable of making good decisions and choices about what he or she will do and how he or she will act in a given situation.

- We all have some things we can do easily and well, and other things that we don't do as well.

- We can become better at things that we choose to spend time practicing.

- Everyone makes mistakes. Mistakes can help us learn.

- Asking questions or not knowing how to do something does not mean one is stupid or dumb; it just means we haven't learned how to do it yet.

- We work best with those we respect and trust; this means we need to be honest and truthful about what we say and do.

- None of us like to be bossed or forced to do things, but we all have responsibilities and goals that we must do. (Students could clarify what they think are included in responsibilities of student and teacher.)

- None of us can do exactly what we want to do all the time. We have to make choices. There are boundaries to help us make better choices and work and live together safely.

CLASSROOM RULES

Rules are broad statements of expected behaviors. The main purpose of rules is to provide a safe and positive environment that will promote positive learning behaviors. In student-centered learning environments, rules set standards for personal responsibilities and interactions.

- School may have sets of expectations (rules) for general use areas (hallways, lunchrooms, etc.) and policies that deal with law issues.

- School may have pledge of statement of expected behaviors; this pledge could substitute for rules. Discuss behaviors that are implied by the pledge.

  — A "Sounds Like," "Looks Like" T chart could be developed for concepts; for example, "treat self and others with respect."

- Who makes the rules in student-centered classrooms? Students will understand why and what is expected if they have a voice in setting the rules.

- The amount of input and method will vary depending on age and experiences of students.

  — State your expectations and rationale for rules.

  — Ask students to brainstorm rules that they think are needed for them to know how to act to be safe learners. (You are also teaching and modeling problem-solving procedures.)

— Write down all student suggestions. Teacher can also add suggestions, especially if students are having problems thinking of relevant ideas.

— Delete all that you or students think would not be appropriate.

— Ask students to combine all suggestions that are alike. This is a good sorting and categorizing activity.

— Condense until there are one to four ideas in number.

— Make certain rules are stated in the positive; they state what students are expected to do.

    – Example: Show respect for self and others.

— For young children, or children who have limited experiences in self-responsibility, clarify and practice:

    – Looks like/sounds like chart

    – Role playing

- Provide visual copy of expected behaviors.

— Posted on wall or bulletin board

— Individual copy; this could be developed as a contract for students

— May integrate with studies; for example, if studying government, could format as the Constitution

PROCEDURES

Procedures are all the "how-to's" that inform students what is going to happen, when, and how; establishing and consistently using procedures will promote effective learning with few interruptions or distracting, off-task behaviors.

- Procedures set the parameters that allows students to function as independent and responsible learners and members of the learning environment.

- Procedures increase learning time by reducing off-task behaviors, "waiting and boredom" spaces.

- Procedures include setting up effective routines to reduce problems and time spent dealing with problem behaviors.

- Defining and learning procedures are among the most important things to be accomplished in first weeks of school.

- Teacher must carefully think through the whole day and all activities and possible situations.

  — Determine when/what times and activities need procedures.

  — Determine what procedure will best meet goals.

  — Teach students these procedures.

  — Students can be involved in setting some procedures. For example, how can they best move from recess to classroom or classroom to lunchroom in efficient and orderly manner that will not interfere with the rights and needs of others?

  — Once procedures are determined and taught, teachers must be consistent in following procedures if they expect students to do same.

- Examples of needed procedures for daily occurrences

  — Entering classroom

  — Exiting classroom

  — Bathroom, drinks

  — Taking roll

  — Lunch orders

  — Collecting money

  — Emergency situations (fire drill, etc.)

  — Dismissal

  — Moving from place to place (to media center, lunchroom, etc.)

- Procedures involving learning materials and supplies

  — Space for students' and teacher's personal materials

  — Group use materials

  — When, who, how materials obtained

  — Who, where, when materials are put away

  — Difference "throw-aways" and recycle materials

- Interaction procedures

  — When/how of listening expectations

— When/response or talking is appropriate

— How to let teacher know student has response or question

— How teacher signals to get attention of student group

- Procedures for students' learning products

    — What required on papers/products (name, date, etc.)

    — Where completed work goes

    — Where/what do with incomplete work at end of work period

    — Make-up work

        – Where/how obtain assignments

        – Due dates

- Teaching-learning procedures

    — Teaching procedures; starting signal, behavior expectations, what teacher will provide

    — How to define individual work space and materials

    — Differences between individual and group work

    — Choosing activity when choices or options are provided

    — How to get help when needed

    — Clean-up signals and expectations

SIGNALS

Many of the procedures may involve signals. Signals are nonverbal methods of communication. Teachers can use their imaginations when developing signals; make them fun when possible.

- Signals to indicate desire to speak or question

    — Raise hand

    — Thumb up

    — Use object such as colored card or cup

    — Technology, when individual student components are provided

- Everyone is expected to be quiet and listening

  — Standing quietly in specified spot

  — Sound pattern (clap, snap, etc., students join in until all are participating)

  — Bell, rain stick, musical tone

  — Posting visual flag or colored light

  — Humorous prop or puppet

- Clean-up time (or—more minutes until end of period)

  — Specified music or song

  — Specific tone or bell

  — Timer (visual and auditory)

- Check yourself to determine if making best choices

  — Any audio or visual cue noted

  — Use of "silly" props, such as glasses with googly eyes

  — Use puppet to look at, sit on shoulder, etc.

  — Focus eyes on student

  — Walk toward and stand by student

- Time for specified learning activity

  — Specified story or music (story time song)

  — Costume or other visual

    – Mark Wittman (K–1 teacher) dons doctor's coat, glasses, stethoscope as Dr. Reading to signal reading lesson and activities

  — Posted daily schedule

    – All classrooms should have specific daily schedule

    – Pictures and clock faces can supplement learning at lower levels

TEACHING PROCEDURES

Students must be taught the procedures that will be used by the teacher and students. Procedures must become a part of the daily routine. Start the first day with procedures that correspond to activities for the day.

- Procedures for first day

    — Entry and exit procedures

    — Roll-taking procedures

    — Seating position

    — Names on magnets; student puts name under appropriate heading; this could include indication of lunch choices, etc.

    — Indicator for speaking

    — Personal materials needed/where stored

    — Procedures to accompany activity of day

- Succeeding days

    — Be consistent in using procedures already taught

    — Add new procedures as needed for activities

    — Daily procedure assessment at beginning of term

        – Student self-assessment form with listed procedures

        – Have students self-assess on personal success

        – Teacher can sign and have student take home

I liked to incorporate literature or songs when I taught procedures. An example of how I taught the "Stop, Look, Listen" procedure to young children included the steps outlined below.

SAMPLE OF TEACHING A PROCEDURE

1. Read a story or poem about ice cream.

2. Have children stand and pretend they are an ice cream cone; have them use their arms to put a scoop of ice cream on top of their cone.

3. Ring bell or chime to indicate ice-cream truck.

4. Practice having the children stand, look at you, and make an ice cream cone each time they hear the bell.

5. Use the signal consistently whenever you want them to stop what they are doing, look at you, and listen for directions.

6

Promoting a Community of Learning

Cooperate—Remember the banana: Every time
it leaves the bunch it gets skinned!
Anonymous

Student-centered classrooms emphasize cooperation and promote learning by working and helping others learn. An atmosphere must be established for these goals to be actualized.

The learning community will function most effectively when

- students and teacher know and accept each other.

- students and teacher trust each other and know mistakes will not be laughed at.

- students and teacher can ask for help from others.

- guidelines are set to help students make responsible choices to benefit self and group.

People are not born knowing how to cooperate and work together. These skills have to be learned through personal experiences. Teachers cannot assume that students have developed these skills in the home or in other educational environments.

SOCIAL SKILLS

Students will need to learn multiple skills for positive social and work interactions.

- Listening skills

- Expressing own ideas and feelings

- Conflict resolution skills

- Praising and encouraging behaviors

- Setting and working toward common goals

- Asking for and accepting help from others

- Celebrating successes of others

- Acceptance of differences in opinions and skills

- Sharing attention, work load, and materials

TEACHING SOCIAL SKILLS

Many teachers feel there is not sufficient time in the day to spend time teaching social skills. Social skills can be integrated within other aspects of the curriculum.

- Coordinated with teaching of procedures and expectations

- As part of process of problem solving and decision making

- As objectives within the existing curriculum

    — Feelings and friends in social studies curriculum

    — Verbal and listening skills of language arts

    — Problem solving and decision making

    — Goal setting and self-assessment

    — Literature/reading focus

    — Business or career education skills

CLASS MEETINGS

Teachers in student-centered classroom often incorporate the use of class meetings. Class meetings provide opportunities for students to have a voice in decisions in the classroom. Class meetings can be integrated with teaching the democratic process (town hall meeting, or formal meetings with Robert's Rules of Order); class meetings can be applications of problem-solving process.

- Teach the process you select with choice or decision students can make in the first days of school (rules, procedure for exiting, etc.).

- Set aside a time for regular class meeting (weekly, alternate weeks).

- Establish procedure for teacher or student to call for meeting for special problem.

- Write agenda; teacher has final decision on agenda topics.

- Agenda items can include problem situations, planning events, or team-building discussions.

- Jobs or responsibilities can be assigned and specified for each meeting (leading, recording, encouraging).

COMMUNICATION SKILLS

Communication skills include the ability to express ideas, feelings, and needs as well as the ability to hear and respond to others. These skills are instrumental for success in all phases and relationships in life. Teachers must be willing to really listen and hear what students are saying. Teachers should model these skills at all times. Students should have the opportunity to practice communication skills in numerous situations beyond an assignment for learning activity.

- Everyone needs to believe that their feelings and ideas have merit.

- Feelings of acceptance must be present for true communication to occur.

- Nonverbal messages are often first messages of acceptance.

- Listening, not talking, is key to good communication.

- Give invitations for student to continue talking ("Mm hmm, interesting, tell me more," etc.).

- Listen for and respond to underlying feelings of message.

- Provide feedback to check or clarify accurate listening of message.

- Never use judgmental "put-down" messages, or attempt to tell speaker what they should do or how they should feel.

- Goal is to facilitate students in finding solutions to their own problems.

TEACH POSITIVE METHODS TO SOLVE DIFFERENCES

Students need to possess methods to relate their feelings, needs, and dislikes, which will expedite positive results. Teachers cannot assume all students have learned these strategies. These skills can be practiced through puppets or role play; discussions and writing may be preferred application methods for older students.

Various methods can empower students to solve problem situations, whether they are minor irritations or all-consuming problems.

- Ignore looks, remarks, and signals intended to send negative messages or "put down" the value of person.

- Move away from persons who initiate nonproductive interactions (put-downs, name-calling).

- Use "I Message" to communicate feelings and needs.

  — This method is very effective when positive caring exists between giver and receiver of message.

  — Message includes:

  I feel (frustrated, concerned, rejected, etc.) when you (behavior want changed) because (why).

  Examples:

  I am very concerned when students do not put materials away in the assigned places, because the next class has to waste their learning time searching for the materials.

  I would really like to hear what you have to say, but that tone (choice of words/volume) hurts my ears. Could you talk in a voice so I can listen to you?

  I am really concerned when you don't follow procedures in the hallways. I'm afraid you or some other student will be injured.

  — Adjust message for developmental level of students. Young students' message could be:

  I feel _____ when you _____. Will you please stop?

  Examples:

  I don't like it when you use my scissors and glue without asking first. Would you please ask when you want to borrow something from me?

  It scares me when you hold on to me when I'm on the monkey bars. Will you please stop?

  — Introductory discussions could identify feelings. A list of emotions can assist students in identifying emotions beyond mad-sad-glad.

  — Model "I messages" and encourage and guide students to use them for appropriate situations.

COOPERATIVE LEARNING

Cooperative learning extends beyond group work.

- Cooperative learning provides structure for every group member to hold an important role or responsibility in the group.

- Cooperative groups have a common role; each team member must contribute to reach the goal.

- Each team member assumes independent accountability. No member can slide by and let other group members do the work and learning.

- Team members must interact and collaborate to share ideas and reach the goal.

- Assessment in cooperative learning activities can involve multiple assessments.

  — Group assessment on a product

  — Individual assessment on an objective

  — Group and/or individual score on affective/cooperation objectives

  — Student self-assessment

GROUP LEARNING STRUCTURES

Teachers will probably want to select two to four group structures for repeated use. These structures can be taught in the first weeks of school in conjunction with team-forming, get-acquainted, or review activities (teaching procedures). Some structures are easily incorporated into all levels and areas of teaching.

- Think Pair Share

  (Developed by Frank Lyman and associates)

  — Problem is posed.

  — Provide time for independent thinking.

  — Share with team member.

  — Share with whole group.

  — Variation: Can have two pairs share, then share with group.

- Heads Together

  — Teams determined (can be predetermined groups or numbered-off groups.

  — Question is posed.

  — Individual think-time allotted.

  — Students put heads together to discuss and make certain everyone knows/agrees on response.

  — Signal or time limit to stop

  — Teacher calls a number; students assigned number in each group must respond.

- Round Robin

  — Team members sit in a circle.

  — Every team member must respond or add to discussion or problem.

- Inside-Outside Circle

  — Students form inside two circles of equal numbers; inside circle faced outward; outside circle faced inward toward partner from inside circle.

  — Each student in one circle has discussion topic, problem, or review question.

  — Students share, discuss, solve problem with partner from inside circle.

  — Students from inside circle rotate to new partner and new problem situation.

  — Discussion situation can be presented; circles rotate to enable students to share with everyone from corresponding circle.

- Jigsaw or Expert Groups

  — Individuals from each group work on one specific area.

    For example, on unit on rain forests: "1's from each group learn about animals from lowest level, 2's next level, etc.

  — Members return to own group and teach other members what they learned in their "jigsaw" group.

  — Group combines learning from all groups to complete project or activity.

Sources for setting up successful group structures, team-building activities, planning, and assessment alternatives are provided by Kagan and Johnson, and Johnson and Holubec.

Johnson, D. W., R. T. Johnson, and E. Johnson Holubec. *Cooperation in the Classroom.* Edina, MN: Interaction Book Co., 1998.

Kagan, S. *Cooperative Learning.* San Clemente, CA: Kagan Cooperative Learning, 1994.

INVITING PARENTS INTO LEARNING COMMUNITY

The optimum condition for learning and growing for every student is when there is strong partnership between home and school. Parents are more inclined to support learning goals of school when they know what is happening at school. There are numerous actions teachers can develop to involve the parents and guardians of students.

- Contact parents early in the year or semester. It is important that first contacts be positive.

  — A phone call, e-mail, postcard or letter could introduce yourself and give a broad overview of what will be happening in your class.

  — Inform parents when and how you can be contacted.

  — Include method(s) you will be using to keep parents informed of activities on continuous basis (newsletter, Web page, bulletin board, or parent center in school).

  — Check to see if you have correct contact numbers and addresses of all parents or guardians who should be contacted or kept informed of each student's progress.

- Determine which informational method will best reach students' parents and guardians; you may need to use a combination (Web page that can be made into hard copy for parents who do not have Web access).

  — Be consistent in keeping information system updated.

  — Include students in construction of news method, if feasible.

  — Be aware that many students will have parents at multiple addresses.

  — Include an invitation (can be in the form of a checklist) to participate in learning for students. Include possibilities at varying levels of involvement.

  — Determine what types of information to include in newsletters. This could include

    – Calendar of upcoming learning events

    – Information about what students have learned

- Information on how learning can be enhanced during non-school times

- Student contributions

- Relevant, high interest topics

• Parent group meetings can be effective methods of meeting parents and furthering understanding between home and school.

— Open-house, Meet Your Child's Teachers, or Spend Time in Your Child's Day are some methods of enticing parents to the learning center.

— These activities can be informal where parents are invited to come in, look around, and chat. Goal for informal meeting is to break ground for establishing a partnership.

— If event is informal, teacher should keep circulating and not be monopolized by one or a few parents.

— Serving refreshments can sometimes attract parents.

— These events could be more structured where goal is to inform and acquaint parents with what and how their children will be learning and the expectations for students. One way to do this is to ask parents to pretend they are the students and have them do a sample of their child's learning experience.

— These events offer opportunities to invite parents to volunteer for further involvement with children's education.

USING VOLUNTEERS IN THE SCHOOL

When parents and grandparents are included in their children's learning community, they become strong supporters of the school, teachers, and of their children's learning. Children understand that school and learning are respected values and accomplishments.

• Encourage family members to volunteer at whatever level they feel they can. Some ways that volunteers can assist on limited or specific basis include:

— Help sponsor field trips or special events

— Furnish or collect materials for special events

— Make learning games or put learning activities together

— Construct needed classroom furnishing (bookcases, stands, etc.)

— Share expertise, special interests, or hobby

— Take active role in parent-teacher school organization

— Be a guest reader for students

- Some may wish to volunteer on a regular basis. This will require some orientation for volunteers.

    — Some volunteers may give individual students one-on-one attention while they listen to students read or practice specific skills or play games to reinforce learning.

    — Volunteers can help with organizational tasks for teachers, putting learning materials and activities together, putting up displays, etc.

    — Some volunteers are comfortable working with small groups. They can be trained to help make certain a specific learning center or activity or to keep center running effectively.

    — Volunteers who work directly with students need to know:

        – Roles they are expected to fulfill (giving directions, questioning, redirecting)

        – Short explanation on your expectations of student learning and behavior and how these help students learn

        – Which behaviors are considered "off-task" or "not acceptable" and how to respond to those behaviors

        – Ethical and confidential requirement, including what to do if not going to be able to come when expected

        – How to encourage students

    — These expectations could be specified and kept in a special handbook for volunteers and substitutes.

RELUCTANT PARENTS

It may be more difficult to entice some parents to get involved with their child's school in any way. This may be due to time constraints or they may not feel comfortable in school environments because of their own past experiences as students. There is also a tendency for parents to become less involved with school and teachers as their children become older (this may also be because their children are less inclined to want parents there).

- Focus on positives about the child. These parents are probably expecting to hear negatives. Show parents that their child is valued and can learn.

- Home visits could be an alternative. Check with the principal to learn if there are any specified policies concerning home visits.

- Phone calls are another alternative, but will need to be conducted when parent is home.

- Dialogue journals or homework trackers that offer space for teacher and parent messages offer opportunities for sharing information on a regular basis.

- Student exhibits or performances are one of the best ways to entice parents. Schools frequently have music and sports performances, or special events like science fairs.

- Teachers can also consider holding "Shares or Celebrations of Learning" where students share what they have been learning in the classroom. These shares would be smaller and offer more opportunity to publicize all student accomplishments and to interact with parents.

- Recruit parents to invite and bring other parents to school events.

- If the teacher and parents speak different languages, an interpreter may be needed.

- Use vocabulary that parents can understand; educational jargon usually communicates little to non-educators.

- Stress idea that teacher and parents are working as partners to help each child grow and learn to the best of their ability.

7

Motivation for Learning

Those who wish to sing always find a song.
Swedish proverb

Tell me and I'll forget.
Show me and I may not remember.
Involve me, and I'll understand.
Confucius

Motivation refers to the drive to do something. Motivation can come from external sources:

- Please another person

- Grades

- Prizes

- Awards

- Treats

- Money

Or from internal sources:

- Personal goal

- Fun or enjoyment

- Interest

- Desire to learn

CULTIVATING INTRINSIC MOTIVATION

The goal in the student-centered classroom is for each student to engage in learning due to internal or intrinsic motivation. The goals, structure, and activities in the student-centered classroom should cultivate intrinsic motivation.

- Goals for lifelong learning require a desire to take actions to learn.

- Students are empowered to be responsible for own decisions and consequences.

- Students are recognized for their individual gifts and abilities.

- Choices are offered in learning activities (method, levels of difficulty, etc.) to promote successful learning by all students.

- Positive environment supports undertaking new experiences and risks.

- Mistakes are viewed as learning opportunities.

- Group interactions and cooperative learning reduces competitive outcomes and prospect of "losing."

- Learning activities reflect student interests.

- Learning activities are relevant and applicable to students.

- Learning activities incorporate authentic, real-life situations.

- Students have choices.

WHY CAN'T I USE REWARDS OR PUNISHMENT?

Does this sound like something you have or would say? "But I liked getting those prizes and rewards." "Punishment worked for me; I was afraid of doing something that would get me in trouble." If so, this section is for you.

- Rewards and punishments are administered by person in power position.

- Conflicts with the goal of having learner having control of their own events.

- Rewards move focus from learning to the reward.

- Students tend to do minimum requirements to receive reward.

- Rewards tend to promote competition.

- Rewards and punishment do not address the reason that undesirable behavior is occurring.

- Effects are short term and restricted to environment issuing punishment or reward.

- External rewards or punishment undermine or decrease intrinsic motivation.

IS THERE EVER A TIME FOR REWARDS?

Do you mean I can never give students a treat or recognition? What if my students have a history of working only for rewards and expect to be rewarded with tangible rewards?
   Rewards appear to have less damaging effects under certain conditions.

- Give treats "just because" without specifying prior or expected conditions or after the fact.

- Give student responsibility for self-monitoring and assessment for deciding if and when a reward is merited or desired.

- Don't turn action into a contest to receive the reward.

- Keep the reward as close as possible to criteria for earning; for example, for reading, it could be a book or extra time for reading rather than food or a toy.

- Celebrate or share success of students by having learners share what they learned and accomplished.

IS THERE A DIFFERENCE BETWEEN PRAISE AND POSITIVE FEEDBACK?

Encouraging words should not be avoided. However, what and how encouragement is given can produce different effects on students and their motivation. Positive feedback provides information for promoting student learning or decisions.

- Avoid empty or phony praise to individual or groups:

  — You are so good.

  — You all did such a good job.

  — I love your work (paper, picture, etc.).

- Avoid praise aimed at having students' actions only to please adult.

- Comment on what student does rather that on what student is as an individual.

- Make the feedback as specific as possible:

  — Your description of your story setting is so clear, I can easily form a picture and feeling in my mind.

— You have thought of a number of good strategies; have you decided which you will use to solve the problem?

— Positive feedback never humiliates or embarrasses students.

• Smiles and other nonverbal positive feedback should be shared frequently and not reserved for students or situations only when student tried to please adult.

SETTING UP LEARNING ACTIVITIES TO PROMOTE INTRINSIC MOTIVATION

So, the goal is not to "force, make, or bribe" students to choose to participate or to make responsible choices. If you are seeing refusal, disinterest, or "do I have to?" attitude, look at your expectations and how they were presented to students.

• What are you expecting students to do?

— Is the activity boring and viewed only as busywork?

— Do students have choices in method of learning and practicing objective?

— Are the activities developmentally appropriate for students?

• How did you communicate your expectations?

— Did student interpret request or assignment as an ultimatum?

— Were directions or expectations presented in clear fashion for students to understand?

— If there were requirements or circumstances that allowed no or little variability, were these explained to students? Were students granted responsibility and ownership for fulfilling requirements?

PROMOTING STUDENT AUTONOMY

The goal in a student-centered environment is for every individual to be self-governing. The goal would be for students to make positive choices that would foster their goals (not just comply with adult requests). This would also imply that students are aware that they had made choices and are therefore responsible for the actions and consequences that result from these decisions.

Autonomy will be promoted when:

- choices are real, not connived or pseudo choices.

- students are encouraged to question and discuss.

- students make decisions.

- students are granted "ownership" of problems and are responsible for solving these problems.

- students can determine best choices; behaviors reflect their rational.

SETTING STUDENT GOALS

Students will display motivation to work toward goals they want to achieve, rather than goals others think they should achieve. Students will be motivated to work toward goals that share common traits.

- Goals should be short term (the younger the student, the more immediate the goal).

- Goals should be specific, so student knows expectations and can determine when goal has been reached.

- Students need to be involved in setting goals.

  — How might teachers help students set realistic, attainable goals?

- Goal setting with students necessitates planning and organization by teachers.

  — Student's individual learning preferences and experiences are considered.

- Teachers must know goals and objectives to be able to help students plan their learning:

  — curriculum guides and goals

  — objective checklists

  — can be preset listing; student and teacher make decisions about projected dates and column for noting when goal met

  — can be separate goal sheet for each subject or learning period

- Young children may write daily or weekly goals from objectives teacher has determined are appropriate for student.

- Students should reflect "why" if previous goals are not met when setting new goals.

- Goals can include independent learning behaviors (completing and turning in completed work) and monitoring of own behaviors or interactions with others.

Sample of Goal Sheet

GOAL PLANS

Name _____ Date _____

Goal Area _____

Goal(s)_____

_____

_____

_____

I plan to have goals met by _____

Date goals completed _____

Self-assessment:

Great job: _____

_____

_____

_____

Like to improve or work on in future goals: _____

_____

_____

Teacher comments: _____

_____

_____

WEEKLY GOAL SHEET

Name _____ Date _____

Learning Goals (may choose to list by subject):

1. _____

2. _____

3. _____

4. _____

Personal/Social Goals:

5. _____

6. _____

Self-assessment: _____

Goals I completed successfully (list the goal number): _____

Goals I need to continue to work on: _____

What I can do to meet these goals next week: _____

_____

_____

Teacher Comments:

_____

_____

_____

8

Promoting and Monitoring Student Choices

Few things help an individual more than to place
responsibility upon him, and to let him know that you trust him.
Booker T. Washington

If you treat an individual . . . as if he were what he ought
to be and could be, he will become what he ought to be and could be.
Goethe

ROLE OF THE TEACHER IN STUDENT-CENTERED ENVIRONMENTS

Because the goal in student-centered classrooms is for students to be both responsible members of the learning environment and successful learners, students have the responsibility of making and following through with choices to meet these goals. Therefore, the role of the teacher is to facilitate student choices and growth.

- The facilitator creates the environment and procedures to help students determine parameters and expectations.

- Facilitators plan learning activities to motivate and cultivate involvement and successful progression of learning.

- Teachers in the facilitator role teach students to use problem-solving procedures to determine best alternatives for their actions.

- The facilitator provides feedback to promote self-evaluation of student choices.

- Teachers listen to students to determine student needs and wants.

- Teachers or trained students may assume the role of mediator to guide students in resolving conflicts.

MONITORING STUDENT BEHAVIOR CHOICES

After the teacher organizes and teaches students the expectations and procedures of the learning environment, the major responsibility of the teacher is then to monitor the learning and interactions. Effective monitoring entails some basic actions of the teacher.

- The teacher must be mobile and circulate among all students.

- Close proximity can offer support for students who require feedback on a more frequent basis.

- Nonverbal communication messages can help student refocus or receive encouraging feedback.

- The teacher can observe and listen to students' learning progress.

- The teacher can ask questions to facilitate student thinking when needed.

- The use of predetermined signals can redirect or help students focus.

FOCUS ON POSITIVES

Humans need and want interactions with others. Feedback from others influences how individuals view "self" and personal capabilities. These personal thoughts and beliefs will, in turn, impact choices of what and how each will respond to specific situations. All students should approach learning with expectations that, with effort and persistence, they can achieve success.

Feedback messages should be presented to promote positive, constructive interactions. Humans need and want interactions from others.

- Avoid comments that demean student and abilities:

   — Ordering

   — Preaching

   — Criticizing

   — Lecturing

   — Blaming

   Give constructive feedback:

   — Focus on effort.

— Invite student to talk and share feelings, questions, or thinking process.

— Respect their feelings.

• Remember to use "I messages" to communicate feelings and needs.

Remember, goals in student-centered, lifelong learning classrooms foster student curiosity, questioning, and critical thinking. These qualities and skills will not be enhanced in an environment that demands compliance from those in power positions. Young people must learn to make decisions about what is right and wrong based on multiple factors of the situation rather than on whether they will gain favors or punishments. To foster the goal that student actions will be based on rational thinking, students must have multiple opportunities to view alternatives, make decisions, and to be responsible for the outcomes of their choices.

INCORPORATING HUMOR

• Humor helps create a comfortable environment for learning.

— Humor helps reduce stress level of students and teachers.

— Humor encourages comfortable environment for students to undertake new challenges and view mistakes as a positive step in learning.

— Humor promotes idea that learning is a fun and enjoyable event.

— Humor can "open" the mind to be more creative.

— Humor can promote vocabulary and rhythm of language.

— Joy and fun need to be shared; thereby, encouraging unity between students.

• Humor is an effective method of reducing tension in the learning environment.

— Humor can be used to help students take a look at personal behaviors without becoming defensive.

— Humor should always be used as a positive (never to ridicule and belittle).

— Teachers can use silly signals with props (hat, nose, puppet, trick, etc.) as signals that student's choice of behavior may be a bit ridiculous and needs to be checked by student.

— Intersperse short "just for fun" breaks to help students take a break and refresh their minds and bodies.

— Many classrooms distractions are caused by students with misdirected humor. Help students redirect their need for play and fun to enhance, rather than detract, from the learning environment.

— Humor can help students focus on positive possibilities instead of pessimistic outlooks.

Resource: Diane Loomans has numerous resources and specific activities for using humor in the classroom.)

INDIVIDUAL STUDENT CUES

Some students may have difficulty making productive choices on a consistent basis. These students may not have had opportunities to develop self-empowerment attitudes and choices, or they may have some problems in focusing and maintaining their attention to completion of task.

- Get to know the student as a person, not a problem behavior.
- Clarify student's strengths in learning strategies.
- Determine social-emotional needs. These needs might include:
  — attention from adults or peers;
  — confirmation of worth as an individual person;
  — validation of ability as learner;
  — control over choices.
- Offer opportunities for student to share thoughts and wishes; these could be either verbal or written.
- Some behaviors may irritate you while students may be unaware of the effects.
  — Try an "I message" for these situations

NONPRODUCTIVE STUDENT CHOICES

Sometimes, students may exhibit behavior choices that generate negative or nonproductive learning for themselves or classmates. This may be a student who consistently has had needs that were not met in home or school or were responded to only when child exhibited negative behavior choices.

- Severe or ongoing behaviors that interfere with positive learning for one or more children are addressed through problem-solving method.

  — The problem-solving procedure would have been taught and used in learning situations, so that the procedure would be familiar to students.

  — The process will be facilitated if the teacher possesses good listening and empathy skills and diagnostic skills.

  — Knowledge about developmental and personal characteristics of students will help teachers guide this process toward successful resolution of the problem situation.

  — The students must be involved in all phases of the problem-solving procedure.

  — The student will need to use thinking skills to objectively look within themselves. It is important that students look at the real cause of their problems.

  — Thinking skills will be enhanced by looking at the problem and determining real solutions.

  — Motivation to follow the plan is enhanced when students have a voice in determining the solution; students also are more likely to accept responsibility for monitoring the plan.

The steps of the problem-solving method of solving behavior problems follows the same problem-solving method used to solve math and science problems. It is a good idea to record the steps in writing (see sample form on pages 54–55).

- **Step 1: Identify and define the problem.**

  — Use active listening to let student "vent" feelings and frustrations before starting the problem-solving method. The problem-solving conference should be scheduled after the student (and teacher) have had the opportunity to "cool down."

  — Teacher needs to listen carefully to try to identify underlying cause of student behavior. It is not always important to have student identify this cause or need.

  — Use "I message" to state own concerns.

  — To guide student in accepting and identifying problem situation, ask nonjudgmental questions:

    – *What did you do?*

    (This may need to be repeated several times to focus on their role in the situation.)

    – *Did your choice of action help meet your goals or needs?*

- Guide student to clarify and state the problem situation. The student must accept that they are empowered to change their behavior.

- **Step 2: Generate possible solutions to solve the problem.**

  — Let child contribute ideas first.

  — Do not judge or evaluate ideas. Accept all solutions.

  — Offer or guide alternatives that will address the underlying cause of behaviors.

  — Offer an alternative or cue to guide or encourage student to promote ideas if student seems to be stuck and doesn't offer alternatives.

- **Step 3: Evaluate alternatives.**

  — Ask student to help pick the solution (or possibly combine solutions) to see which will best solve the problem.

  — Help student look at complications or possible consequences of the alternatives.

  — Teachers should be honest and veto alternatives that do not meet their needs or comfort level.

- **Step 4: Decide on the best solution.**

  — Ask student to test out solutions left after step 3. Ask questions like, "Do you think you could follow through with this idea? Do you think it would really solve the problem?"

  — Let student pick a solution to try. Let student know you are willing to do your part if he or she is committed to do their part.

  — Write down the plan. Be specific on exactly what the student and you have agreed to do.

  — Be specific about dates, times, and places of the plan.

  — Each person should sign the agreement to show their commitment to following and plan and solving the problem.

- **Step 5: Implement the plan.**

  — Give a copy of the plan to student and teacher (parent could also receive copy if parent was involved).

— Develop a monitoring system so plan is consistently followed. Student should have a principal role in the monitoring of the plan.

— Teacher must be consistent in following the plan if student is expected to follow the plan.

- **Step 6: Follow-Up Evaluation**

  — Follow-up should be consistent. Ask student if the plan is working for him or her.

  — Teacher and student may determine that the plan needs to be modified. Modification may be realized as result of living out the plan, or teacher and student may need to return to possible solutions in step 4.

Sample student plan

INDIVIDUAL STUDENT PLAN

Name _____ Date _____

Events that you responded to; what feeling/emotion were you experiencing?

_____

_____

_____

What did you do?

_____

_____

_____

What were the results of this choice?

_____

_____

_____

Did this meet your goals and needs?

_____

_____

_____

What were some alternative choices?

_____

_____

_____

Which choice will you choose if situation occurs again?

_____

_____

_____

What cues will help you follow your plan?

_____

_____

_____

I pledge to follow my plan and make choices that will result in positive outcomes.

Student _____

I/We agree to follow student's plan _____

Monitor date _____

Check date _____

(For Primary)

MY PLAN

Name _____ Date _____

What did you do?

_____

_____

_____

Did your choice of behavior help you?

_____

_____

_____

What other choices could you have made?

_____

_____

_____

What will you do the next time you have to make a choice?

_____

_____

_____

How will you remember to follow your new plan?

_____

_____

_____

9

Planning for Successful Learning for All Students

What we have to learn to do, we learn by doing.
Aristotle

The ultimate goal in the classroom is for all students to be successful learners. When students are involved and are successful learners, intrinsic motivation is almost guaranteed. Positive involvement in learning also diminishes the probability of off-task and task-avoidance behaviors.

PLANNING FOR SUCCESSFUL LEARNING

Planning learning goals and activities for all students to be successful and continuous learners is a major role for the teacher in student-centered learning classrooms. Students should be involved in the planning process. The level of involvement will vary depending on comfort levels of teachers and developmental levels of students.

Where does one start in this planning process? It is *not* a matter of just opening the text and doing the next page, running off lots of worksheets, or finding cute or showy activities that will look good on display. The first part of planning is discovering standards of expectations of student learning.

- Look at state standards or expected outcomes. States may vary in standards or expectations; some may focus on strategies and skills, while others may be very specific in the information and topics that students are expected to master. Any required state assessments should correspond to state standards or stated expectations. One can start with the standards and then plan, or plan and work backward to document objectives and methods used to meet the standards.

- Ask to have a copy for the school district's curriculums and goals. These should include expected learning goals and objectives. Check to determine if district goals correspond to state expectations. Your school administrator should provide you with these guides and additional information concerning expected outcomes.

- Talk to, and work with, teachers on your team or level. Many teachers work on teams in the planning process. Schools may have previously defined some parameters; this could include themes at each level. Planning with team members is a definite plus for beginning teachers or teachers who are new in the school.

YEARLY OVERVIEW

It is helpful for planning purposes to know the broad scope and sequence for the year. One will then be able to order or begin collecting the materials and resources for learning units.

- Is there a unifying theme to tie the whole year together?

- Look for a theme that helps organize learning for students.

- Examples include relationships, families, patterns, cycles.

- What units will best support learning goals and objectives?

- Are there topics or specific types of information mandated by curriculums?

- Are there topics that will be of high interest to students? Particular interests and passions for students and teachers can encourage deeper investigation. This is a great place to engage students' input. Individual or group conferences, check sheets, and interest surveys might be used to facilitate this process.

- Fewer number of units allows more time to spend learning at greater depths of knowledge and application.

- Are there any important local issues or problems in which students might want to become involved?

- Look for natural sequencing of objectives and topics.

- How can subject areas be integrated? Look beyond the normal, restricted ties.

LONG-RANGE PLANNING WORKSHEET

When: _____ Who: _____

Overall Theme or Focus: 1

QUARTERLY LONG-RANGE PLANS

School Year: _____ Group: _____ Teacher: _____

Organizing Theme: _____

Theme: Main Goals: Focus Concepts: Authentic Tie-ins:	Theme: Main Goals: Focus Concepts: Authentic Tie-ins:
Theme: Main Goals: Focus Concepts: Authentic Tie-ins:	Theme: Main Goals: Focus Concepts: Authentic Tie-ins:
Theme: Main Goals: Focus Concepts: Authentic Tie-ins:	Theme: Main Goals: Focus Concepts: Authentic Tie-ins:

UNIT PLANNING WORKSHEET*

Theme: _____

Objectives	Content Concepts	Process Activities
Subject Integration	Assessments	Resources

*Recommendation: Enlarge chart, photocopy to 8½"× 14" page, with six columns across page.
This form will probably work best for upper levels.

Planning the Unit

Unit plans extend beyond the goals and themes; unit plans identify main concepts and skills students will learn in the unit. Plan the main activities in which students will be engaged in learning these concepts and skills; you might wish to plan by types of activities, processing skills or subject areas. Procure ideas from students; offer choices and alternative methods that students can use to learn and demonstrate learning. Think about the resources that will be needed for the unit and, finally, what assessment methods will best determine whether students have learned the identified concepts and skills.

You may find it more convenient to complete the Pre-Planning Worksheet, and then expand the unit planning on the computer; this elaborated form will facilitate your daily/weekly lesson planning.

PLANNING WORKSHEET FOR THEME ACTIVITIES

Theme: _____

Disciplines	Reading	Writing-Listening	Social Studies	Science	Other
Content Concepts					
Skills					
Authentic Real-Life Connections					
Resources					

PLANNING SHEET FOR UNIT INTEGRATED ACTIVITIES

Theme: _____

_____

Reading   Listening-Writing

Social Studies   Science-Health

Math   Technology-Art-Music-P.E.

CONTENT AREA UNIT ACTIVITIES PLAN

Theme: _____

Activities	Information Gathering	Investigative	Resources
Content Concepts			
Skills			
Authentic and Ties to Other Classes			

WEEKLY PLANS

Weekly plans are the most detailed plans. These plans should provide guidance for the teacher when planning and preparing learning objectives and activities. Weekly plans can be documentation for accountability on meeting learning expectations.

WHAT SHOULD BE INCLUDED IN WEEKLY PLANS?

- There are multiple lesson-planning formats; some are very sketchy and provide only page numbers or main activity of students. Minimum required components of plans should include:

  — *Objectives* students will learn and be able to perform upon completion of learning activities.

    – Objectives should consider cognitive, affective, and actions.

    – Format that facilitates learning needs of all students includes writing the broader learning goal, then specifying objectives to include range of student goals.

  Objective: Money: Can recognize and use money coins

    – Can name the coins and their value

    – Can count coins to 25 cents

    – Can count coins to $1.00

    – Can do operations (add, subtract) with money

    – Can make change to $1.00

- *Materials and resources* required for teaching-learning activities. Put this in format that can be easily checked during prep time.

- *Procedures*, which include several components and may be done in list form.

  — Introduction: how the concept or activity will be introduced to students (how to tie in to prior experiences, excite and entice, and make relevant and meaningful to students.

  — Questions that may instigate students' critical or creative thinking.

  — Small or large group seminar: what you and students will do during if this is a portion of teaching-learning process.

— Activities in which students will engage to understand and apply learning objectives. Options for varying levels and methods of learning would be included here.

- *Assessment* includes methods in which students will demonstrate success in meeting learning objectives. Assessment methods directly reflect learning objectives and teaching methods.

  — Responses to questions and observation of students during learning activities may be forms of formative assessment.

  — Include any products students are asked to complete.

  — Processes can be documented by pictures or student drawings with captions, student logs or journals, or teacher or student documentation in response to set criteria.

  — Student self-assessments can rate product or process of learning. Rubrics or checklists guide this process.

HOW DOES THIS FIT IN THOSE LITTLE BOXES IN TEACHER-PLAN BOOK?

It won't! But neither do the plans need to be as detailed as those required during your methods classes. Lesson plans document and guide what will be done and be a component in teacher accountability and reflection processes.

- Use a computer to format lesson plans. Hard copies can be stored in loose-leaf binders if one chooses or needs hard copies. Daily/weekly schedules could be separate page/insert. This is particularly useful when writing plans for objectives/activities that extend beyond one day.

- Activities that are included in the daily or weekly schedule (opening, story share, journal) will basically need few changes every week. Don't forget the daily/weekly schedule. The schedule should be posted so students will be able to learn to monitor time.

- Enclosed is a form one could use for handwritten plans. If you use a computer to record lesson plans, an elongated written form with headings could be used.

- Lesson plans are developed for specific objectives, but the activities may expand over the entire week. It is not always necessary to write a separate plan for each day; the steps and sequence of activity can be noted on one plan. This allows for some flexibility in time requirements for different students.

LESSON PLANS

Lesson _____ Theme _____

Date(s) _____ Teacher _____

Objectives	Strategies, Groupings	Materials, Resources	Assessment
What will they learn?	How will they learn?	What will be needed to learn?	How will they show they have learned?

SUBSTITUTE PLANS

Professional teachers strive to be present on a regular and consistent basis, but there are legitimate reasons for occasionally not being in the classroom. The teacher is still responsible for planning and organizing learning for the classroom. If the absence is unplanned, emergency substitute plans can be a lifesaver.

- Prepare the emergency plans early in the year; update as necessary.

- Make certain the principal or another teacher knows where to find your regular and emergency plans.

- Remember that the substitute may be a person who has never been in your class—or in a class with goals and structure similar to yours. In many places, substitutes have had little or no teacher training.

- Talk to your students prior to being absent. This could be a general "if I'm ever not here" expectations, share when you know you will be absent. Students almost always test substitutes (sometimes, this is just a reaction because they are upset by the change); try to avoid this by communicating how you trust their ability to make choices that show respect to all and demonstrate their intelligence and self-regulation.

What should you include in the substitute plans? Think about what you would want to know if you were walking into a new learning environment for a short time.

- Include copy of weekly schedule. Include explanation of any extra duties and responsibilities they are to assume.

- Include class role and procedure for taking role.

- Share any specific information about a student only if that information is vital for student's daily success.

- Be specific about learning group memberships (who/where, etc). Specify when/how talking and sharing is expected.

- Explain the expectations of students and procedures developed and practiced that enables students to meet those expectations.

- Put in copy of daily activities (copies from lesson plans).

- Include an activity that can be initiated for emergency basis that could replace or supplement part of your weekly plans. A literature book with follow-up activity; thinking and skills-reinforcement games are also handy inclusions. If students have had exposure to, and are familiar with, these types of activities, success is more likely.

- Include names of persons who can be contacted for explanations and assistance: team members, volunteers, and students who are responsible for specific procedures and learning teams.

- A copy of school lay-out, where to find teachers' rest room, lunch room, telephone, etc. is helpful.

ORGANIZERS TO FACILITATE STUDENT LEARNING

Some students have not developed organizational strategies that tie previous learning to new information, determine patterns and relationships between concepts, and gain meaning and understanding of concepts. These students then attempt to just memorize; they may be able to repeat or give the information back in the memorized form, but will have great difficulty in tasks that require application or using it in a different way. Therefore, providing these students with organizational methods and strategies can provide the foundation to tie concepts together and structure follow-through activities.

Multiple organizers have been developed by educators. You can determine several methods that correspond to concepts and activities used most frequently in your students' learning. These organizers can then be easily adapted to fit specific learning tasks. After using these organizers for specific lessons, provide students with copies (or enlarge and post) and encourage students to use them for independent projects.

Graphic organizers help students by:

- providing visual representation of ideas

- showing relationship of concepts

- helping organize ideas to promote understanding and remembering

- promoting ability to apply and expand concept ideas

- fostering divergent thinking

KWL CHART

What I Know	What I Want to Know	What I Learned

The **KWL** Chart is a very functional method to help structure learning for a unit of study. The teacher can make a big copy on chart paper; this stays up during the whole unit. This is a good way to introduce the use of the chart for all ages, and will undoubtedly be the preferred method for young children. After demonstrating and using the method whole group, older students can be provided with a copy and can complete it individually or in learning groups.

The **KWL** organizer is great for introducing a new topic or unit. The **K** component, *what I already know about the concept,* can readily determine students' prior knowledge about a topic or can assist them in seeing the relevance of their prior knowledge. It can also serve as a pre-test to let the teacher determine if students have sufficient knowledge and experience to understand a concept, and the differences of background between students. This will provide the teacher the knowledge to plan the range of activities for all the students to be successful and continued learners.

The **W** component is *what do want to learn?* about the concept or topic. This encourages students to get involved in their learning and making the learning relevant to students. Motivation to learn is enhanced when students are learning because they want to know, rather than because an adult is telling them they need to know. Questions are necessities in discovery learning and in implementing the scientific process of learning.

The final **L** is the assessment portion of the learning. It shows if students' prior knowledge was correct and whether they found the answers to the questions posed in the **W** component. Again, this can be an individual or group activity.

A fourth column could be added to guide students in determining the answers to their questions. If the column was added on regular-size paper, the fourth "what I learned" column could be added to the back of the paper.

What I Know	What I Want to Know	Resources to Discover	What I Learned

KWL

Name _____ Topic _____

Date _____

K	W	L
What do I know?	What do I want to know?	What did I learn?

KWL EXTENSION

An extension/variation of the **KWL** is to have students make a factual individual book about the concept using the statements in the **K** portion of the chart.

- Page 1:   Statement of what student thinks or knows about the concept.
              Fact or fiction? (or true or false?)

- Page 2:   Tell whether statement was true or false; add details to support. Add illustration or graphic.

- Page 3:   Repeat process from page one with another statement taken from K portion of chart. True or false?

- Continue using statements and results of research and learning until book is complete. Add title pages, cover, etc., for a finished book.

- The statements can originate from individual students for individual books over different areas of a broad concept. Books can then be presented and read by class members as a sharing/teaching method by students.

- Younger children could do group chart; statements could be printed on odd-numbered pages in preconstructed book, and children could complete the information and picture on even-numbered pages.

SPIDER OR ATTRIBUTE WEBS

Spider webs can visually organize attributes about a specific concept.

- Teachers can model uses of spider webs during problem-solving brainstorming sessions by grouping responses while recording students' responses.

- Webs help students group ideas as a pre-writing exercise. Students can then visually see how to paragraph their ideas. Adding headings over each group of ideas provides information students can use for topic sentences.

- Attribute webs can have one circle with a theme or topic with "leg" describing things about the topic.

- Attribute webs can have the main topic with subtopics; the subtopics can then have describing attributes.

    — For example, an attribute web about reptiles could have attribute legs that describe characteristics of reptiles.

— The attribute web with the reptile theme could have one leg with reptile characteristics and another with examples. The example circle could extend to name animals that are reptiles with an additional circle to distinguish how the families of reptiles are different.

Attribute or Spider Webs

CIRCLE WEBS

Circle webs are similar to spider webs; the topic of concept is in the middle, with pie sections around the middle. The number of sections can be adjusted to fit the concept or assigned task. Circle webs could also be used for concepts that are continuous: seasons, months, life cycles, etc.

Title _____   Name _____

Title

_____

Sequence Map

Title _____   Name _____

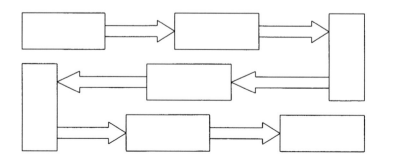

SEQUENCE MAP

Sequence maps or chains are methods to graphically show the sequence of events. This could be the sequence of events of a story; happenings in a person's life; life cycles; steps in any process.

LIFE LINES

Life lines are a great way for students to organize significant events in a time sequence:

- Organize significant events of own life
- Sequence life of historical persons
- Sequence historical events

Sequence Chart

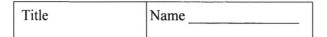

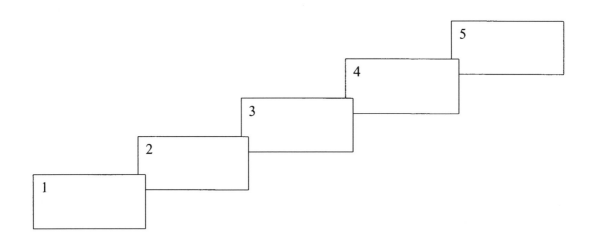

CLASSIFICATION MATRIX

A classification matrix is helpful in showing examples of specified characteristics. A classification matrix can be used with any subject or topic area:

- Compare costs of items from different outlets

- Compare stories' characteristics

- Organize criteria to determine problem solutions

- Organize and compare historical events

Sample:

CHARACTERISTICS OF FOLKTALES

Story Titles	Sets of 3	Magic	"Bad" Character	Happy Ending

VENN DIAGRAMS

Venn diagrams are useful for sorting and comparing activities. The number of circles can vary from one, three, or four. Actual circles (plastic, yarn or ropes, bent coat hangers) can make circles to sort real manipulatives or items.

- One circle could be used to sort yes/no characteristics of concept.

- Two and three circles are ways to sort and organize attributes items to show characteristics that are different and those that are shared.

Venn Diagrams

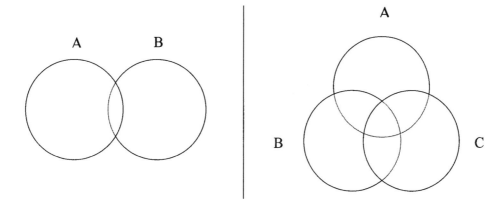

RANKING LADDERS

Ranking ladders are visual graphs to show order or ranking:

- of cause of event

- of importance of person or event

- order of completion or finish

- most significant causes

- solutions to a problem

Ranking Ladder

Topic _____

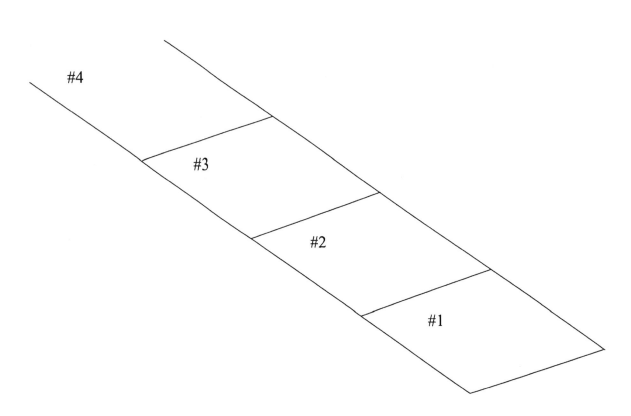

HERRINGBONE

Herringbones visualize the subparts of a particular event:

- Sequencing of historical events.

- Sequence of problems in stories.

- Who-where-what-why components of real or fictional events.

- Help students organize ideas to create the events to solve the problem before writing a story.

Herringbone

Topic _____

Main Idea

DECISION-MAKING GRAPHIC

The decision-making graph could be the chart that students complete to resolve personal problems experienced in the learning environment. It could also be used for problem solving in math, science, and other situations that involve the problem-solving model.

Problem-solving Matrix

Problem:				

Solutions

Decision:				

CAUSE-EFFECT VISUAL

Cause and effect are common objectives in all subject areas and in social interactions of students. Numerous graphics can be developed to help students organize thoughts and events to determine causes and effects:

- To identify problem and contributing factors in solving students' personal and social problems

- To identify causes of historical events

- To pinpoint ideas in scientific experiments

- To determine actions in story events

Cause-Effect Visual

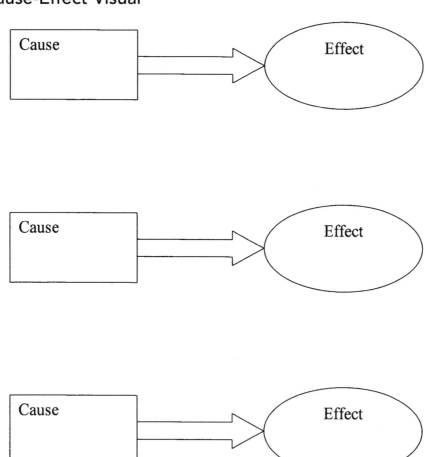

FIVE W'S CHART

The five W's (who, what, where, when, why) or the four W's and how have several uses:

- Prewriting for factual events
- Describing historical events

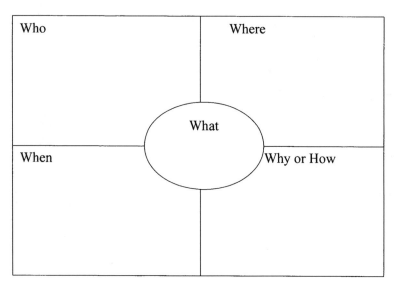

5 W's + Historical Chart

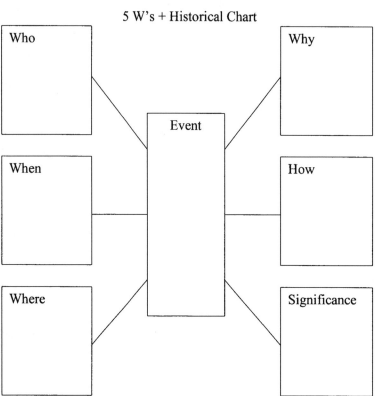

STORY MAPS

Story maps can help students in the organization and comprehension of stories as well as pre-writing component before writing their own stories.

- Young children may find the sequence of "Character name," "wanted," or "wanted to" (goal), "but" (problem), "so" (what did to resolve problem), "until" (solution).

- More accomplished writers can be encouraged to have continued complications, or several steps or solutions to attempt before resolving the problem.

- Encourage writers to include characteristics of the character so the reader can better identify with the character(s).

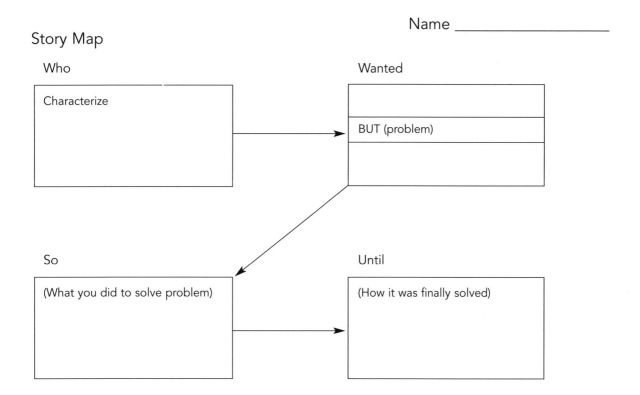

Story Map   Name _____

Who   Wanted

Characterize

BUT (problem)

So   Until

(What you did to solve problem)   (How it was finally solved)

SELF MAP

Self maps are methods to help students look at themselves and facilitate setting of future goals.

- Self maps could easily be incorporated into the math curriculum. Students could design their own figure map with pattern pieces or other shape manipulatives. Shapes could be drawn around to make an individual map.

- Older children could be asked to make shapes of specified sizes and shapes (name shape, length of side or parameter or area of shape).

- Shapes and labels can be changed to identify areas students should reflect on about themselves.

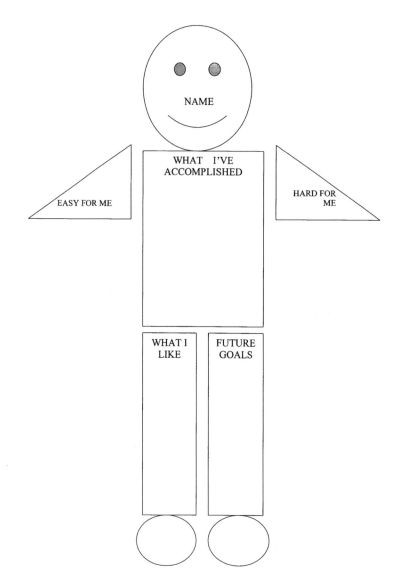

IMPLEMENTING LEARNING ACTIVITIES

Meeting All Students' Needs

The majority of students make the most significant progress when working in small heterogeneous groupings of students. Teachers will likely use numerous groupings at different times for a variety of reasons.

- Although most groupings will be heterogeneous, homogeneous groups may be used for some purposes and activities.

- Groupings should be flexible. Subgroups should change periodically to meet varying rates of development and achievement.

- Special care should be given so no group is labeled or recognized as substandard. Avoid names or labels that may imply merit or worth.

Grouping Strategies

- Teachers use numerous groupings to facilitate student interactions and learning.

  — Individual situations

    – Solve social problem

    – Planning group

  — Ability levels

    – Should be for specific purpose for short period of time

    – Could be for specific "skill needs" seminar

  — Interest centers

  — Hobby or special activity groups

  — Learning styles

  — Topic area

  — Cultural or language

    – Same

    – Mixed

  — Class meetings

— Peer teaching groups

- Students need to be taught responsibilities and skills for demonstrating, cueing, encouraging

- Peer tutors can be mixed age-grade or same age-grade

- Students needing practice with a skill can tutor younger or less experienced students

- Children who tutor and those being tutored both make significant gains in learning

— Cooperative groups

- Heterogeneous ability groups of three to six

- Elementary groups are gender mixed

- Middle and secondary may be gender mixed or same gender

- Consider personality and learning strengths and differences

- Cooperative groups have names, individual and group responsibilities

- Cooperative groups are usually together four plus weeks

MEETING STUDENT DIFFERENCES

Choices for multiple methods of practicing skills and demonstrating competency should be provided. Real life integrations and applications, learning and cognitive styles, and differences in intellectual strengths will help guide inclusion of multiple opportunities of learning.

• Opportunities to discuss and brainstorm with others can be facilitated by using any of the multiple grouping strategies.

• Include body-kinesetic methods. Most young children have difficulty sitting still for longer than five to 10 minutes (older students can probably double the time).

— Include large muscle activities (drawing/writing on mural, boards, etc., instead of small, lined paper)

— Work areas should have places to sit on floor, lounge areas, etc.

— Include drama, pantomime, dance, role play; demonstrate skills and concepts

— Include stretch or movement break activities as needed

- Music and rhythms can enhance learning for most students, add interest, enhance memory recall.

  — Incorporate piggyback songs:

    - Can be developed by teacher or students

    - Brainstorm ideas about concept

    - Incorporate melody from old standard

    - Fit words to chosen melody

    - Can add simple instrument accompaniment

Sample developed by Tamara Padfield, pre-service elementary education student at Fort Hays State University, Hays, Kansas, for a fourth-grade class.

MEASUREMENT SONG
Sung to tune of The Flintstones

Measurement, let's learn about measurement.
It's a number followed by a unit.

The **English** units of length
Are **inch**, **foot**, **yard**, and a **mile**.

The **inch** is the smallest of them all,
The size of your thumbnail to your knuckle.

Now let's move to feet.
It's next in size and they sometimes stink.

The **foot** has 12 inches in all.
It's about the size of a football.

Next is the yard.
It's quite smaller than the distance to Mars.

The **yard** contains three feet or 36 inches.
The length of a baseball bat.

Finally is the mile.
It's the biggest unit in this song.

One **mile** is 5,280 feet.
Just think, about four times around the block.

Measurement, let's learn about measurement.
It's a lot of fun, you'll see . . .
Oh yes, you'll see. . . .
It's fun for you and me!!

YEAH!!!!

ADDITIONAL RESOURCES FOR SONGS

Cloonan, Kathryn. *Sing Me a Story—Read Me a Song (Books 1 and II)*. Beverly Hills, FL: Rhythm & Reading Resources, 1991.

Dulabaum, Gary. Amber Circle Music. New Orleans, LA: Juliahouse.

- Use songs from different historical eras as basis for studying history:
  - Adds high interest for students.
  - Songs reflect issues of the time.
  - Encourages students to create own songs to reflect their concerns and/or learning.
- Rhythms and tempo enhance learning of facts and basic knowledge:
  - Rap can be developed by pre-adolescents and adolescents.
  - Children can clap, snap, tap, stomp rhythms to accompany words and aid memory.
- Visuals and technology promotes teaching and learning:
  - Expand learning opportunities:
    - Obtain information
    - Practice concepts
    - Demonstrate learning
    - Assessment
  - Equipment and materials:
    - Computers and printers
    - Video cameras
    - Audio recorders and players
    - Basic materials: blank paper, cutters, methods to put together
    - Display boards
    - Calculators

— Technology changes rapidly and may be expensive:

- Grant monies are available for purchase and inclusion of technology.

- Teaming and integration heightens probability for grants.

— Levels of reading materials:

- Students will have multiple reading levels.

- Resources and learning materials should be available at different levels.

- Teacher presentations/shares will benefit students with lower reading levels.

• Develop learning centers or modules:

— Learning centers and modules promote independent responsibility:

- Objectives, directions, accountability/assessment methods included.

- Introduce activities and procedures so students can be independently successfully.

- Activities can be independent or group.

- Centers and modules can be used for all ages and skill levels.

- Centers and modules can be main or supplemental method of student learning.

- Provide tools (scoopers, sweeper) to facilitate clean-up.

— Offer multiple activities for learning and practicing objectives:

- Develop activities at varying concept and skill levels.

- Include variety of manipulatives.

- Self-checks and accountability/assessment methods included.

- Develop management system to assign or have students self-select center choice and rotation.

- Multiple resources include activities and plans teachers have developed; some sources include Creative Teaching Press; Scholastic; and Bureau of Education and Research; Crystal Springs Books; and Center for Innovations in Education.

• Other helpful hints:

— Storage for learning center activities when space is limited:

- Portable stacked drawers, labeled by topic

- Ziploc bags

- Paper bag center activities

- Baskets or buckets

- Covered shoeboxes

- Plastic peanut butter jars

— Define work area and facilitate use of materials for individuals:

- Laminated flat paper mats (minimum 12″ × 18″)

- Cookie sheets or pizza pans (great with magnets)

- Carpet samples

- Microwave meals' plastic containers

- Plastic containers to hold pencils, etc.

— Helpful supplies with multiple purposes:

- Rolls of magnetic tape; can be cut to any size and can make almost anything magnetic (charts, attendance, games)

- See-through, reusable colored emphasizing tape

- Various stamps (can have self-inking); messages could include: date, work in progress, first draft, "this belongs to . . ."

- Packets of ring closures to hold pages for big books, charts, etc.

- Multiple three-ring notebooks

- Three-ring hole punch

- File holders that are accessible to students

"Junk" items you may solicit from parents or local businesses:

Paper

- Scraps or ends of papers (printing companies are a great resource)
- Wrapping paper and ribbons
- Old wallpaper sample books
- Bags (those with handles are especially useful)

Boxes and Cardboard

- Lightweight cardboard for book covers
- Thick cardboard for displays and projects
- Empty paper roll holders (tissue, paper towel, wrapping paper)

Magazines, Catalogs, and Newspapers

- Be specific about the type of magazine you want (like old copies of *Ranger Rick*, travel magazines, state promotional magazines, etc.)
- Newspapers for specific projects

Sewing Items

- Material scraps and pieces
- Ribbons, trims, etc.
- Large eye needles and thread

Other

- Eye droppers
- Straws
- Boxes of toothpicks
- Old dice
- Film canisters
- Plastic containers and jar with lids
- Microwave meal plates
- Cookie sheets and trays
- Old measuring cups and spoons
- Wrapped knives, forks, and spoons
- Magnets

10

Monitoring and Assessing Student Learning

Whether you think you can or think you can't, you're right.
Henry Ford

This chapter will focus on the role of assessment in the student centered learning classrooms. Assessment is one component of the teaching-learning process, so it provides feedback to facilitate this process. Learning and assessment are both continuous and simultaneous processes. The assessment methods supply information for students and teacher to assess progress toward learning goals.

MONITORING AND FACILITATING LEARNING

- Keep students interested and involved in their learning:

  — Is the topic and objective relevant to students? Do students see a reason for exerting their time and effort to learn?

  — Have you offered choices?

    – Choices may be in practicing and learning objective, or in product, materials, or method to demonstrate their learning

    – Example: Can activity be independent or group?

      ○ Can practice be on computer, with game, practice paper?

      ○ Can product to show understanding be a demonstration or performance?

      ○ Does student have choice of oral or written?

      ○ Does student have topic options? For example, if objective was to compose a paragraph with topic sentence and supporting detail sentences, were students allowed to pick topic for their paragraph?

- Do students have individual learning goals?

  — If students have been involved in setting individual goals that have immediate dates for completion, then students are more inclined to work toward meeting those goals.

  — The less mature the student, the more immediate the goals.

- Are you consistent in using your established procedures?

- Are you mobile and aware of what is going on in the classroom?

  — Your physical nearness or eye contact can be reminders for students to check what they are doing.

- Do you ask questions or give probes to instigate further thinking and action by students?

  Examples:

  — Your puppy sounds great; can you tell about some things you like to do with your new puppy?

  — What do you think will happen if you add more drops of water?

- Do you give positive feedback to recognize acceptable behavior or good work?

  Examples:

  — I really like the way you organized your problem; it makes it easy to follow your thinking process.

  — You've shared many good ideas; does anyone else have a different way to solve the problem?

ASSESSING STUDENT LEARNING

Assessment is a part of the teaching-learning process. Assessment is directly tied to the learning objectives; assessment should demonstrate if the learning objective has been met. Assessment is a broad concept; it expands beyond the concepts of testing and grading.

Because learning in the student-centered classroom features dynamic, authentic activities with the focus on the learning processes, assessment should feature these same features. This chapter will examine methods of ongoing formative assessments and ways to document student learning. Summarizing and sharing student learning methods of portfolios, "grade" reports, and conferencing will also be shared.

In the student-centered classroom, students are involved in the assessment process.

- Students should know the goal and how they will be assessed.

- Students should know the criteria for levels of success.

- Self-assessment should be an instrumental component of student learning process. Students should be able to monitor progress toward individual goals.

FORMATIVE ASSESSMENT PROCESSES

Formative assessment takes place on an ongoing basis; the purpose is to determine if students understand concept currently being taught or applied. The purpose of formative assessment is not to grade; the purpose is principally to determine if adjustments should be made in learning activities to facilitate student learning. Formative assessment will be most beneficial if students are involved and aware of needs for successful learning.

FORMATIVE ASSESSMENT METHODS

- Observation of students' work, demonstrations, and body language:

  — Walk around the classroom to establish physical proximity with all students.

  — Be aware of any indicators that students may be experiencing learning blocks (facial or body expressions, off-task or avoidance behaviors).

  — Give specific and positive feedback messages.

    "You remembered to start all your sentences with capital letters. Great job!"

    "Your selection of describing words really helps us identify with the character."

- Responses to questions:

  Ask questions to help lead students to the next step of the process or self-correcting procedures. Examples of questions:

  — Work the problem out loud; tell why you decided to use this process.

  — Does that explanation make sense? How can you change it to make your explanation clearer and easier to understand?

- Practice problems:

  — Again, help students verbalize what they are attempting to do.

— Determine if they need assistance with the process or if the errors are in the application.

— Learning is enhanced if corrections are made immediately rather than waiting until the teacher takes papers, marks errors, and returns to student at later time.

— Quality, rather than quantity, of student work should be stressed. Therefore, quality should be considered in assigning goals and activities for students. Make certain students understand that effort should focus on completing assignments *the best they can*, rather than doing more in a hurried, mediocre way.

• Rough draft of proposal of process being learned:

— Students need to learn that perfection is not expected the first time someone tries a process, but improvement is expected at each step. Improvement should reflect learning of the student.

• Student learning and improvement will be geared to each student's level. Some students may begin at higher levels than others, but all students are expected to show growth in their learning processes.

• Help students formulate a plan or outline for completing the process or project.

• Model concept of putting down initial ideas (may result from brainstorming process) to get started on a project; demonstrate how mistakes and revisions can be made.

— Erasure is NOT recommended; student and teacher should be able to follow students' learning process.

— Mark one line across part to be revised; write new version above old.

— Use caret to add insertions (these can numbered and added at bottom of paper or on another paper).

— Young children can cover errors with computer address labels and write correction over the label.

— If using computers for composing, run copies at various stages to show progress.

— Chart to show editing methods can be posted in classroom (grades two and up).

ASSESSMENT DOCUMENTATION METHODS

There are numerous ways to document formative learning. Responsibility for documentation is not solely placed on the teacher. Students are involved in numerous documentation methods.

CHECKLISTS

Checklists are lists of specific objectives of learning. They are usually subject or process specific. Checklists can be compiled on individual student basis or by groups.

- Checklist of learning objectives:

  — Observation dates should be included.

  — Symbols for levels of competency can be delineated (introduced, progressing, mastery).

  — Student and teacher can be responsible for individual checklist dates (could be component of student individual assessment).

  — Group or class checklists are the responsibility of the teacher (these can be kept on clipboards for easy access).

  — Teacher can document learning during observation-facilitation periods.

See samples on pages 110 and 111.

SELF-EVALUATION

- A student's self-assessment is a component of individual goals. Students need opportunities to view themselves in noncompetitive and nonjudgmental conditions.

- Focus should be on individual behaviors and performances (what he/she actually did); then relate to future goals.

- Self-assessments will be most successful as impetus to learning if students know and understand criteria for assessment; rating scales or rubrics are helpful tools to guide student learning and assessment.

- Students at all levels can learn to effectively use self-assessment. The number of choices and methods of recording the assessment must fit the developmental ability of the students.

— Young children may have choice of *yes/no* or mark *smiley/frowny* face.

— Options or levels of performance can increase with ability to self-reflect.

See sample on page 112.

PEER EVALUATION

• Peer assessment is most appropriate in cooperative learning situations and should accompany self-evaluations. Peer assessment can specify individual responsibilities and contributions to the group.

— Rubrics of expected responsibilities assist students in assessing group members objectively.

— Students can also state what/how the group was most successful and set goals for improvement.

See sample on page 113.

ANECDOTAL RECORDS

• Anecdotal records are recordings of actual events (who, where, when, what). These incidents might include:

— Specific typical learning example

— Specific typical behavior

— Specific atypical behavior

— Language sample

— Humorous incident

— Exact details of suspected abuse or students' disclosure of abuse

• Anecdotal records should be jotted down immediately for most accurate recording. Some find it helpful to fold the paper in half; write short, contextual observation on the left side; then, later, write reflection or follow-through comments on the right side.

Anecdotal records can be used for all levels, but are most often used in early childhood situations. Anecdotal records can be part of the total assessment program or only for specific types of behaviors and incidents.

- If part of total assessment program, recorder need week by week observation plan to document behaviors of all children:

  — All observations must be dated

  — Focus on only a few minutes of interaction

  — Note if typical or atypical behavior

  — Should be recording or factual events

  — Verbal samplings could be recorded and transcribed to record actual pronunciation, vocabulary, or oral reading behaviors

  — Videotaping of incident (check school policy on uses beyond classroom)

- How should anecdotal information be used? Incidents should be stored in the student's portfolio and combined with other data for assessment purposes, to:

  — Provide basis for further observations or assessments

  — Share atypical incidents with parents and other professionals working with child for advice and insight

  — Provide opportunity for discussion with child to gain additional information or to formulate plan

  — Provide evidence for Child Protective Services

  — Provide basis for curriculum planning (group or individual)

See sample on page 112.

RUBRIC ASSESSMENT GUIDES

Rubrics are tools that specify expectations of the learning process or product. Rubrics include criteria for different levels of competency.

- The content of rubrics provides a focus for teachers' planning and instruction:

  — Rubrics can be developed for specific products or performances or long-term developmental skills.

— Rubrics can be developed to assess development of a process.

— Rubrics expedite reliability of assessment.

- Students can use rubric specification to guide learning and performance:

    — Specific behaviors direct and guide students' self-assessment.

    — Rubrics facilitate parent understanding of student learning expectations.

- Rubrics can be adapted from existing rubrics (See Taggart, G. L., S. J. Phifer, J. A. Nixon, and M. Wood (eds.), *Rubrics: A Handbook for Construction and Use*, Lancaster, PA: Technomic Publishing Co., 1998, for samples and more specific details on development and use).

- Rubrics can be developed by teachers or cooperatively by teacher and students.

    — Number of levels, descriptions of expectations, and form can be adapted to meet developmental and ability levels of students.

    — Three or five levels are most common.

    — Students may need to view samples of work at different levels to describe differences in expectations.

    — It is usually easier to start the development of descriptors at beginning or exemplary levels, then develop the middle level(s).

    — Use positive terms to describe all expectations (describe what did rather than what didn't do).

    — One can be creative in descriptive terms that designate different levels (On Launchpad, Lift-off, Soaring); descriptive terms can correspond to topic of assessment.

See samples on pages 115–116.

SUMMATIVE ASSESSMENT: GRADING OR SUMMARY OF COMPETENCY ACHIEVEMENT

Eventually, student learning will require some type of summative assessment that describes student progress for students, parents, and other interested audiences. Parents and summations for other/future teachers should include detailed information to promote continuous growth and learning.

- Summative assessments summations derive from many components:

    — Teacher observations (checklists, anecdotal records, etc.)

    — Progress in application of learning processes (problem solving, decoding unknown words, estimations, predictions, cooperative learning, etc.). Progress could be noted by descriptions or by checklists or rubrics.

    — Student self-assessments

    — Student performances and demonstrations

    — Student-produced learning products (problems, writings, models, webs, pictures, etc.)

    — Teacher-made tests

    — Commercially produced assessments

- Summative assessment should reflect student achievement in relation to teaching-learning objectives.

- Summative assessments should correspond to teaching-learning activities.

- Summative assessment methods should be developmentally appropriate.

- Summative assessment methods should be multidimensional and reflect the overall picture of student learning behaviors and achievements.

- Remember that every problem or piece of student work completed by students during the formative learning process needs to be included in the summative assessment.

- Should homework be considered in summative assessment? Teachers need to consider several issues in making this decision.

    — Was the purpose of the homework to determine whether student could independently apply skills or concepts? If homework is considered independent practice, then progress should be noted as formative, rather summative assessment.

    — Did all students have access to resources to enable them to successfully complete the homework assignment? Teachers should consider developmental as well as students' home environmental factors (access to materials, assistance, support).

    — Students must know that all learning activities are important in their learning progression. Therefore, homework is not just busywork, and "grade" should not be emphasized.

SUMMARY AND DISPERSION METHODS

- Achievement results summarized and dispersed to interested persons in various ways. Teachers should check with school policies to determine which, if any, are required by the school. The most common methods include:

  — Portfolios

  — Conferences

  — Student demonstration of competencies

  — Narratives of goals and successes in meeting those goals

  — Checklists of objectives mastered (may include levels of mastery or exposure to objectives)

  — Letters or numbers to represent bands of success of completed work

  — Percentage of work successfully completed

  — Combinations of any of the above

- A single grade or score is the least preferred method. Although this method has a history of use and acceptance, there are a number of problems with this method:

  — Grade bands vary with teachers and schools.

  — There is no description of what student completed to receive grade.

  — Does not tell whether grade is norm (compared with others in class) or criteria referenced (compared to objectives).

  — Grade inflation is common in all levels and schools.

  — Grades tend to focus student interest and motivation on the grade rather than on learning.

  — Grades tend to reduce the challenge to undertake challenging learning goals.

- The best method of providing students' progress should provide information or feedback to students, parents, and other educators to make decisions about students' learning programs.

- Progress should be criterion-referenced; that is, it should be based on learning goals and objectives.

PORTFOLIOS

Portfolios are useful assessment tools in student-centered learning. Portfolios represent a collaborative approach to assessment while allowing for individual differences between students.

- Portfolios should include samples to represent students' progress of learning goals. Some key ingredients of portfolio assessment include:

  — Students have ownership of their portfolios; they should help decide contents of the portfolio.

  — Goals are for portfolio to represent students' evolving work and foster self-evaluation.

  — Contents show students' strengths, needs, and progress.

  — Two portfolios are recommended. The "working portfolio" is the collection of work by both teacher and student. Items are selected from the working portfolio that represent objectives and student achievement for the final portfolio.

  — Specific criteria (i.e., rubrics) for evaluation of samples is included.

  — Students' self-assessments and teacher reflections accompany each final selection.

  — Parent input can be included.

  — Portfolios can be organized around local or state standards.

  — Portfolios can contain developmental checklists of separate subject achievement.

  — Portfolios facilitate conferencing (student-teacher and student-teacher-parent).

  — Transferring portfolios to computer discs facilitates storage and transfer to next school levels.

CONFERENCES

Conferencing is a method of sharing student progress. Conferences in student-centered approaches would focus on student goals and progress:

  — Conferences would include student, teacher(s), and parents or guardians.

  — Conferences would be led by the student.

  — Student would share individual learning goals, then explain or share learning artifacts that demonstrate progress or proficiency.

— Student would use materials from learning portfolios to explain and verify progress.

— Conferences would be finalized by sharing new goals, methods, and resources to assist student in meeting goals.

STANDARDIZED TESTS

- Standardized tests are tests that are developed and distributed by test companies. Their main purpose is to compare test results of a student or group of students with others in the same grade who have previously taken the test.

    — The objectives do not necessarily match classroom teaching-learning goals.

    — Assessment format is usually timed with a multiple-choice format (which doesn't usually correspond to classroom methods).

    — Standardized test results should support what teacher already knows about the learner.

    — Standardized tests may not be efficient in time and cost factors.

    — Results may be available after a lengthy time span.

    — Testing scores may be misunderstood or misinterpreted by parents and public and by some educators.

- Teachers and schools need to consider several issues in making a decision about using standardized tests as a component of the assessment program.

    — Will the results provide useful information about the learners or teaching-learning program?

    — How will the results be used?

    — Who will have access to the results?

    — Are any tests required by the district or state for any student or group of students?

    — Does the test include discriminating items or formats for your students? Are the items or topics and language familiar to the students?

- If the decision is made that standardized tests will be given to students, teachers should take several steps to help prepare students for the tests.

    — *DO NOT* teach to the test. The test is *not a curriculum guide.*

— Familiarize students with the test format. (It probably does not correspond to assessment formats that students typically use in student-centered learning.) Use practice tests provided by test company or developed by teacher for this purpose.

— Familiarize students with language used in test-taking directions. Directions are standardized, but the meaning may not be interpreted in the same way by students. For example, the "best" or "correct" way to say something in a language test may be interpreted by the student as "the best way to say it in my culture," not necessarily the standard English of the test.

— Make certain students know that the tests will include items that they will not know. Students are familiar with assessment in which they have had previous learning experiences; therefore, they assume they should be able to respond to all or most questions. Standardized tests provide a wide range of difficulty; most students will not "know" the answers to all questions.

— Teach students to look for cues to help make best choices. Many of the techniques they have learned about estimation, prediction, and problem solving can be helpful in taking standardized tests.

— Keeping one's place or marking responses on separate sheets can cause problems for students. Make certain they have markers/methods to eliminate confusion.

— Familiarize students with purpose of the test. Students need to be motivated to try to do their best, but not to the extent of accelerating stress levels that will limit their success.

REFERENCES

Taggart, G. L., S. J. Phifer, J. A. Nixon, and M. Wood (eds.). (1998). *Rubrics: A Handbook for Construction and Use*. Lancaster, PA: Technomic Publishing Co., 1998.

CHECKLIST

Checklists for Individual Students:

Student: _____

Observer: _____

M = mastered (can do and explain independently)
P = progressing (needs cues, makes some errors)
I = beginning stages
0 = not yet working toward

Objectives: Observation Dates

CHECKLIST FOR GROUP OF STUDENTS

Observation Date: _____ Observer: _____

Observation Key:　M = mastered (can do and explain independently)
　　　　　　　　　P = progressing (needs cues, makes some errors)
　　　　　　　　　I = beginning stages
　　　　　　　　　0 = not yet working toward

Students　　　　　　　　Objectives

ANECDOTAL RECORD FORM

Student: _____

Activity: _____

Date: _____

Observer: _____

Observation:

Self-Evaluations:

Self-Evaluation for Primary Writing:

Name: _____

Date: _____

Look at your writing. Circle word (yes or no) that best describes your work.

My sentences make sense.	Yes	No
I left finger spaces between words.	Yes	No
I started sentences with capital letters.	Yes	No
I put a . or a? at the end of sentences.	Yes	No

Put a * by goal for your next writing.

Include Writing Process Self-Assessment Rubric from Taggart, G. L., S. J. Phifer, J. A. Nixon, and M. Wood (eds.), *Rubrics: A Handbook for Construction and Use*, Lancaster, PA: Technomic Publishing Co., 1998, p. 64.

PEER EVALUATIONS

Cooperative Group Work for Primary

Team: _____

Did we each do our own job?   Yes   No

Did we praise good ideas?   Yes   No

Did we share ideas?   Yes   No

Did we complete our project?   Yes   No

Cooperative Group Work for Upper Elementary

Name: _____ Team: _____
Date: _____

Circle the response that best describes your team.

1. My team had clear goals for our work.	Yes	Somewhat	No
2. My team stayed on task.	Yes	Somewhat	No
3. We listened and considered each team member's ideas.	Yes	Somewhat	No
4. My team made progress toward our goal.	Yes	Somewhat	No

Circle the response that best describes your behaviors.

1. I listened to everyone's ideas.	Yes	Somewhat	No
2. I offered useful ideas and suggestions.	Yes	Somewhat	No
3. I did my share of the work.	Yes	Somewhat	No
4. I treated all team members with respect.	Yes	Somewhat	No

My Suggestions for Improvement:

Peer Evaluation from T. J. Trout; middle-school science class

PEER EVALUATION

Name: _____

Date: _____

Class Period: _____

Topic/Assignment: _____

Team Members:

A. _____ B. _____

C. _____ D. _____

Use the pie chart to describe the amount of work that each member of your team, including you, completed. *Be sure to label your chart.*

(Insert circle here)

Use the "Rubric for Activities" to describe the color you feel your group has earned.

Color: _____

One thing my group could have done to improve its performance is:

_____

_____

_____

_____

T. J. Trout's Rubric for Activities

Rubric for Activities

Red   No Participation

Orange   Student participation was nonbeneficial to group goals.

                Student behaviors were off-task or inappropriate.

                Student input was incorrect or irrelevant.

                Student may not have understood the goal or problem.

Green   Student behaviors demonstrated minimal understanding.

                Student input provided some insight, but thought processes may have been

                incomplete or not totally correct.

Blue   Students participated in a positive manner.

                All members were involved and contributed.

                Team arrived at the desired outcome/goal.

Purple   Students demonstrated effort beyond expectations.

                Student input was invaluable to the activity.

                Team exceeded proposed outcome/goal.

WRITING PROCESS

Color in the smiley face or the sad face after reading each question below to show how you feel about your writing.

Editing My Writing

Did I check for a capital at the start of each sentence?

Did I check for a capital on all proper nouns?

Did I check for commas between town and state, dates, and words in a list?

Do I have a complete thought in each of my sentences?

Do I have two sentences running together as one?

Do I have an ending mark after each sentence?

Did I check to see if words were spelled correctly?

Source: Taggart, G. L., S. J. Phifer, J. A. Nixon, and M. Wood (eds.), *Rubrics: A Handbook for Construction and Use*, Lancaster, PA: Technomic Publishing Co., 1998.

11

Professional Development

*It is one of the most beautiful compensations
of this life that no man can sincerely
try to help another without helping himself.*
Ralph Waldo Emerson

. . . I find that the harder I work, the more luck I have.
Thomas Jefferson

LIFELONG LEARNER

Teachers are lifelong learners; teacher and learner should be dual roles that teachers in learning-centered classrooms model every day. Teachers must be willing to take leadership roles that extend beyond their own classrooms or learning environments. Teachers who take leadership roles in total school environment and curriculum have influence on professional development of other teachers.

TEACHERS WORK COOPERATIVELY

There are a number of advantages and benefits for teachers who work cooperatively with other teachers:

- More perspectives and expertise are shared and considered with a group; consequently, better decisions can be made.

- Teachers can offer support for one another and offer relief from high stress factors.

- Teachers readily acknowledge that they get most of their good ideas from other teachers; teachers who really care about education of all students readily share ideas and materials with other teachers.

WAYS OF COOPERATING

Ways of teaming range from casual exchanges to sharing in all aspects of teaching-learning. Teaming can occur at all levels throughout the educational system. Many teachers team to make the major decisions about student learning in their level or group.

- Team planning can occur at all levels from preschool up. Teams may be by grade of developmental level; middle and upper school teachers may team by subject area, or have multiple subject areas team to work with a specified group of students.

- Information can be shared and decisions made about almost anything:

    — Curriculum decision for own students

    — Curriculum planning across education program

    — Selecting teaching-learning themes

    — Coordinating resources and supplies

    — Coordinating schedules and duties

    — Planning yearly/unit/weekly lesson plans

    — Sharing areas of expertise and interests

    — Sharing/solving problems situations

    — Looking at learning alternatives for individual students

- Teachers can also team for teaching-leading learning activities:

    — Teaming of two teachers for group of students full-time. This is most common in early childhood settings or regular education where two teachers with different specialties work with all children in the class.

    — Some schools offer opportunities for teaming where two or more teachers work on part-time schedule with students.

    — Students may be grouped by specific needs, interests, or learning levels for part of the day. Or, one teacher may teach social studies and another science to students of both classes.

    — Teachers can teach by subject areas or specific areas of expertise.

    — Teachers who spend the majority of time working with students on math, science, language, and social studies topics can team with teachers with expertise in art, music, technology, media, and physical education.

MONITORING PERSONAL TEACHING EFFECTIVENESS

Teachers must be able to identify areas in which they wish to grow. Individuals will expand personal and professional knowledge and skills most when the individual teacher is involved in identifying and monitoring that growth. This requires the ability to look at oneself objectively and reflect on what happened and its effects. Reflection is a skill teachers need to develop.

DETERMINING AREAS FOR GROWTH

- One must accept that there are areas and skills in which one can become more proficient and effective. These might involve specific situations that occur during the day which foster stress or frustration, or lead to nonproductive results for teacher or students.

- One might also consider investigating new strategies for teaching-learning, methods of integrating learning (i.e., technology programs), or making learning activities more relevant and applicable to students' lives.

- Videotaping oneself is another good method to help identify specific types of behaviors or skills that one may wish to improve. One might also ask an observer (another teacher or administrator) or observe for specific areas you identify.

SETTING PERSONAL GOALS

One to four goals are probably a feasible number of goals in one year. Some goals may be subdivided and consequently require more time and documentation to show growth.

SETTING GOALS

- Some schools may use individual goals as a component, or the main method of assessment of teacher proficiency and development; if so, there is a system of development and documentation suggested.

  — Personal goals areas may include:

    – Planning to meet learning needs of *all* students. This could include determining needs, locating resources, determining relevant, meaningful activities, and how to plan numerous levels and methods to meet specific objectives.

— Developing teaching-learning strategies and techniques could be the major focus:

- Methods to introduce and excite students about learning and refresh prior knowledge

- Questioning skills to promote deeper thinking and understanding

- Providing organizational learning strategies

- Developing methods to engage students in meaningful learning (centers, real-life integration)

- Giving helpful feedback, and designing meaningful assessment

— Setting up and leading a positive learning environment might be the area on which beginning teachers may focus:

- Include setting up procedures and schedules

- Redirecting to encourage student responsibility

- Teaching social skills

- Promote student responsibility in problem situations

— Professional development includes growing in knowledge and skills that extend beyond working with students:

- Could include self-growth and personal organization

- Expand family communications and interactions

- Involvement in school or district interactions and committees

- Grow professionally by taking an active role in professional organizations, workshops, or classes

• Be very specific in stating your goals. This may be stated as a long-term goal for the year; you can break the goal down into subgoals with shorter time lines for completion.

DEVELOPING GROWTH PLAN

• Develop a plan of activities and actions you will take to meet your goal; include projected dates, costs, etc.

• List your projected resources; this includes any persons, information, interactions and meetings, and equipment and supplies you project you will use to meet your goals.

Resources could include:

— Observing or consulting with other teachers. This could include e-mail interactions.

— Attending professional meetings, conferences, conventions

— Taking workshops or graduate classes on specified areas of goal

— Locating relevant Web sites pertaining to growth area

• Determine how you will document growth toward final completion of goals. This could include a reflection journal, video documentation, discussions and observations of others, etc.

REFLECTING AND MONITORING YOUR PLAN

Reflection is essential for growth; therefore, each must find or make the time for constructive reflection. At the end of the day, one may just want to forget about what didn't go right and move on. While the goal is always to focus on positives, one must acknowledge areas that need improvement for development to occur. Where and how can teachers make time for reflection?

• After realizing that an occurrence could be improved, reflecting about the event can indicate possible alternatives for improvement.

• Sometimes, adjustments or better approaches to promote learning can occur during the learning event. Jot these alternatives on the lesson plan so adjustments can be made in future plans.

• If a learning or behavior is complex and ongoing, documentation about what has been attempted and results are essential.

— Not only will documentation assist you in determining what to do, it will also be helpful for consultation with another professional for possible alternatives.

— You might choose to sit down for a few minutes, during a break or after students are gone, for reflection and documentation.

— Document any contacts or discussions with parents and other educators.

• If learning or behavior has already resulted in goal statement or individual contract with student, reflection of both student and adult and documentation can be incorporated with student conference.

- A quieter time away from the setting may be more conducive for productive reflection.

  — Some alternatives for reflection include during the commute to/from work or during a daily walk.

  — To record ideas, keep a small hand-held recorder handy.

- Know yourself; designate a time for reflection that will be most productive. Determine documentation method, *then do it!*

MAINTAINING A PROFESSIONAL PORTFOLIO

You probably created a professional vita and portfolio at completion of your training program; the portfolio was a tool for seeking a professional position. Professional portfolios may be an instrumental component of professional development and advancement.

- Some districts or states may include professional portfolios for professional certification or licensor. Check required documented elements; this would be a good guide when considering professional goals.

- Candidates seeking national certification must assemble a portfolio.

About the Author

I was raised on a ranch in Nebraska and attended small schools for my elementary and high school years. I attended the University of Nebraska in Lincoln and earned bachelor's, master's, and specialist degrees and finally a Ph.D. in educational psychology. I have experience teaching children in their early childhood and elementary through middle school years, in schools in Nebraska and Virginia, and in teacher training programs in Nebraska, Virginia, and Kansas. I'm now living in Colorado.

Hobbies and interests include reading and doing puzzles, and raising, arranging, and photographing flowers. I also enjoy going on nature "investigations" with my husband and our little pug, and taking historical and antique jaunts with our daughter.